Archive of Style

Archive
of Style

New and Selected Poems

Cheryl Clarke

TriQuarterly Books / Northwestern University Press
Evanston, Illinois

TriQuarterly Books
Northwestern University Press
www.nupress.northwestern.edu

Poems in the "Selected Poems" section of this book appeared in slightly different versions
in their respective original volumes: *Targets* (Bushel Editions, 2018); *By My Precise Haircut*
(Word Works, 2016); "The Days of Good Looks: 2000–2005," part 5 of *The Days of
Good Looks: The Prose and Poetry of Cheryl Clarke, 1980 to 2005* (Carroll and Graf, 2006);
Experimental Love (Firebrand Books, 1993); *Humid Pitch* (Firebrand Books, 1989); *Living
as a Lesbian* (Firebrand Books, 1986); and *Narratives: poems in the tradition of black women*
(Kitchen Table: Women of Color Press, 1982).

Many of these same poems were also anthologized in *The Days of Good Looks: The Prose and
Poetry of Cheryl Clarke, 1980 to 2005*.

Printed in the United States of America

10 9 8 7 6 5 4 3 2 1

Library of Congress Cataloging-in-Publication Data

Names: Clarke, Cheryl, 1947– author.
Title: Archive of style : new and selected poems / Cheryl Clarke.
Description: Evanston, Illinois : TriQuarterly Books/Northwestern University Press, 2024.
Identifiers: LCCN 2024013898 | ISBN 9780810147607 (cloth) | ISBN 9780810147614
   (ebook)
Subjects: LCSH: African American women—Poetry. | African American lesbians—Poetry. |
   African American feminists—Poetry. | LCGFT: Poetry.
Classification: LCC PS3553.L314 A73 2024 | DDC 811/.54—dc23/eng/20240402
LC record available at https://lccn.loc.gov/2024013898

To the memory of Gwendolyn Brooks and
Audre Lorde, my friends and mentors

CONTENTS

New Poems

Selected Poems

Narratives: poems in the tradition of black women (1982)

New Poems

PREFACE

I am happy to put *Archive of Style: New and Selected Poems* before you, my readers, who have followed my poetry since the late seventies. My hope with the new poems is that I have ventured into a more contemporary landscape while maintaining my old lenses—by which I mean my ways of seeing sexuality, lesbianism, blackness, African American culture, and narrative expression.

In this section, I reprise my familiar poetic themes. South Africa has always been a resonant motif, thus the opening poem, "Jo'burg, 2016," evokes the country's tortured past through its description of the Apartheid Museum's most "striking" exhibit. Readers will recognize here my long preoccupation with South Africa and the connections to my older poems "Mandela: 12-5-2013" (*By My Precise Haircut*) and "Dreams of South Africa" (*The Days of Good Looks*).

Sexuality received unrelenting devotion in my collection *Living as a Lesbian*. Because of the book's popularity, since 1986, I continue purposefully to make sex and sexual desire integral themes. "Cost" and "Spring 2022" resonate with older poems like "Brief Interval" (2019), "lipstick corny" (2019), "Rondeau" (1993), and "living as a lesbian on the make" (1986). The Queen, Aretha Franklin, appears in two of the new poems, "Never Any Proof" and "Back Seat." She is a force of poetry.

"Signs of the Times," "Sandy Bland," and "Mother Emanuel Nine: their influence was wide" reaffirm my commitment to writing poetry that calls out the continuing peril of living as a black person in the United States—and anywhere else in the world. Readers have witnessed this theme in poems such as "On Their Way to Life" (2019), "oh, memory fateful and fatal" (2016), and "Movement" (1993).

As I continue to write poetry, I remain dedicated to producing work that penetrates the margins of the lives of lesbians, black people, and women.

Jo'burg, 2016

Zee, my young friend, a Jo'burg native with a Steve Biko face
accompanied me as my guide to the Apartheid Museum
at the behest of a comrade.

Like me, Zee had never been to the museum.
Entrance tickets: *Blanke. Nie-Blanke.* Luckily,
we both got *Nie-Blanke* tickets.
So, we saw the exhibits together,
we paralleled and parroted each other's movements
and approached with care the many small exhibits.

One striking exhibit:
The Room of 131 Nooses signifying anti-apartheid fighters—ANC,
PAC, SWAPO, UDF, MK—executed or assassinated for their resistance
   during the struggle:

> Tortured to death, beaten in detention, hanged, asphyxiated,
> buried alive, burned to death, bomb detonated
> in an opened parcel, shot five times
> in the head.

Executions officially ended in 1989.
Few assassins prosecuted.

Never Any Proof

Rev. Clarence LaVaughn Franklin did
anything but protect your mother, though
rumor has it you, Clarence,
her firstborn, are Rev. C. L.'s son
(and grandson)
—and a whole mess in Detroit:

such legend looming over you all your life
    like the Hanging Gardens of Nineveh
        and your mother never confirming
            or denying

just that Sam Cooke was not your father.

Directory Entry

C_____T_____C_____, negro,
b. 1936, Wash., DC

draughtsman,

discharged Air Force 1958 dishonorably.

Easter Mass

A 'Mass' is something you say on Good Friday,
after we walk the Stations for the last time.
The radiologist will
tell me the same thing or not:
'Appears to be a carcinoma.'

Appears?

Back Seat

Last-minute tickets entering back seat of custom cream-colored Lincoln 'Mark'
something-or-other. Maybe it wasn't a 'Mark.' But it *was* Lincoln. Or was it
    a Cadillac?
No, it was a Lincoln.

FM beaming Marvin from dashboard and brown-skin brothers in camel-colored
cashmere and blue and mauve silk neckscarves passing us joints and thermos of cold
Harvey's from front.

We are good and cooked on our way to the Queen's show at Arena. Upon arrival,
cashmere, blue, mauve, and silk brothers split from us to their seats a row from the
Queen's stage. Hand in hand we climb to our upper circle tier to await her.

The Queen and her Back-Ups appear in yellow togas right arms exposed.
The Queen's gold trimmed and she sings sweetly not for very long,
swaying in one spot for the duration,
covering her Back-Ups,
and taking no cues from her band.

We reenter plush back seat and pass remainder of contraband among us for
    return ride.
Only interrupted by lights of a Maryland state trooper.
'License and registration, please, sir. Where you folks coming from?'

'Retha at the 'Rena. Where else?' our driver responds, salty.

All of us thinking *Why the fuck would we even be on this fucking road?*
                'Wish I coulda been there. I'm a real fan of the Queen.'
He bestows ticket to curses streaming out of our noses. Us thinking:
                You can't be a 'real fan' of the Queen if you giving us this ticket.
                'Good evening, folks. Smells good in here. Watch your speed, sir.
                Nice car.'
He pats the driver's door, tips his hat, and backs away.
Send in the frogs.

Betty Carter

(1929–1998)

Turns to face her bassist
magical Betty Carter
in concert in DC the weekend
following JFK's assassination:
in backless
white satin
fitted gown
tiny back bow low
above the gown's split
breaks into her hallmark
'Moonlight in Vermont.'

Slices air with her hand,
'70 in Brooklyn sporting a 'bebop' cap
tries to cut Rashid Ali from covering her.
Rashid will not be cut
(*by some old canary trying to tell me how to play my drums*),
with Betty snapping, 'uh one, uh two, uh one-two-three'
pushing Rashid to brushes
and a real behind-the-beat
'Clang, clang, clang went the trolley'
erupts from her throat.

Late '79 at Seventh Ave. South
complains her pianist is late
in long-sleeve black mesh dress
hair regular black woman style
permanent or cold curl.
Pianist arrives, a woman.
Rolls and scrolls microphone in her palms,
lips flatten against her face
holding her C-note on long *i*:
'Open the door . . . why-*i-i-i-i* make me beg.'

The message

After Papa's heart attack he was the same mean ole bastard to me and Mama he always was sick or well, drunk or sober. Mama say, 'Be patient.' 'Be impatient,' I say.

—MY DIARY

'I'm impatient.
Babygirl, I'm ready to run away with you. With us.
I been calling you. The car
is all gassed.
I got all the magic
and cash (Papa keep in his top drawer)
we need for nine hours of driving.
Break your piggy bank.
Put your license in your wallet.
Be outside, Babygirl.
I'm coming for you.
Can't double park long. Be brave.
As long as we together
we be strong
as the eagle elephant hippo python Kodiak bear.
Pack light.
Wear your winter coat.
I'm coming right
now, Babygirl.
Can't turn back,
no matter that Firebird your mamma promise
if you just be square.
Nor Mastercard.
Bring two pairs of shoes.
Remember your meds.
I'm calling.
I'm coming.
Be waiting for me, Babygirl.
Outside.
Outside.'

Cost

Loving cost you only the synapse
in your brain's absence of sense
and glut of romance.
Slap your head, full of naughts,
tally your thoughts.
Just as well you understand the hooks and
limits.

Remember that last husband?

Stay away from the outdoorswoman on
those weird world-famous bikes,
Olympic skis carving turns.
Get a grip.
Grow up.
Grope your own kind.

Signs of the Times

GEORGE FLOYD'S LIFE
M-A-T-T-E-R-E-D

> Defund the POLICE Defend
> BLACK
> > PEOPLE

QUEERS
Against
RACISM

> BLACK LIVES
> MATTER

SAY *HER* NAME:
BREONNA TAYLOR
SANDRA BLAND

BREONNA TAYLOR
SANDRA BLAND:
SAY *HER* NAME

> GEORGE FLOYD * TAMIR RICE * MICHAEL BROWN *
> ERIC GARNER * BREONNA TAYLOR * PHILANDO
> CASTILE * TRAYVON

> BLACK FUTURES
> MATTER

> P ! O ! W ! E ! R !

George Floyd . . . victim of
our other DEADLY
EPIDEMIC
>How many
WEREN'T
FILMED

I'M NOT BLACK
>*BUT I SEE YOU*
I'M NOT BLACK
>*BUT I HEAR YOU*
I'M NOT BLACK
>*BUT I WILL STAND WITH YOU*

>*IGNORANCE ALLIED with*
>*POWER*
>*IS THE MOST FEROCIOUS*
>*ENEMY JUSTICE*
>*CAN HAVE . . .*   James Baldwin

We *hear* YOU!

>White people:
>JUST
>L I S T E N.

>I AM
HOMELESS
A BUCK
>PLEASE

Sandy Bland

(1987–2015)

i.

Five years, Sandy, since you met your nasty fate.
Writing about you again.
Continue to draw me to you?
Still in your twenties.
Hanged/hung by your neck on a plastic bag in your jail cell.
You'd had your fill of summonses for being a black woman driving a car anywhere in the
United States. Another white dude in blue tailing you looking for that needle-in-a-haystack
infraction was the fricking limit. Let him impale his prick with that same bare bodkin when he
finds it.

ii.

'*Get out of the car now or I'm going to remove you.*'

'And I'm calling my lawyer.'

'*I'm going to yank you out of here.* (Reaches inside the car for you, Sandy.) *Get out of the car.*'

Don'ttouchme!Don'ttouchme!I'mnotunderarrestyoudon'thavetherighttotakeme

'*You* are *under arrest!*'

'Why am I being apprehended?   You just opened my car door!'

'*I'm giving you a lawful order. I'm going to drag you out of here. Get out. Now. Get out of the car!*' (Yanks you out of the car.)

'For a failure to signal? You're doing all of this for a failure to signal?!'

'*Get over there.*'

'You are such a pussy.
You are such a pussy.'

iii.

(Sergeant, woman officer, black, responds to the call for backup and to you,
    Sandy.)
'*No, you are* the pussy. *You should not be fighting. Get on the ground!*'

Speaking past the sergeant, Sandy harangues on:
'Don't it make you feel real good. A female for a traffic ticket. You're a real
man now.'

Cursing him to the neighborhood: 'You motherfucker. You just slammed me,
knocked my head into the ground. I got epilepsy.'

'*Good.*'
'Good?'

iv.

Sandy, you know this will not end well.
He's too far into the deep end now, Sandy,
to pull himself out. (So he drags you down with him.)

Three days and a deluge of sobbing later
your tall brown-skin body
hangs from its avoidable death
in your cell
at the end of a plastic bag.

I Love You, Love You Anyhow

Can't stand it cuz you put me down

I could use a good ole r&b lyric
right about now to face this hard absence.
Only its terse verse can approximate
the testament.

Or the big arms of 'these arms'
circling my wide waist
to close the space
after all the years
            of absence
these big arms
         once more
              once more
to close the space.

I could use a good ole r&b lyric
right about now to face this hard absence.
Only its terse verse can approximate
the testament.

Missed Love

i. no-bra rule

The 'no-bra rule' was one expression of prison authoritarianism—and guards run amok. Women were not into wearing bras then. (I definitely did not wear one, except when I came to the *inside*.)

I was on the inside teaching my writing class, the day the message came up from the gate that Hatti was not allowed inside because she was 'not wearing *her* bra'. All the guards knew Hatti was 'going with' Ahmed, a member of her writing class, and one of the leaders of BIA (Black Inmates Alliance), also the editor of *Lion Lines*, BIA's newspaper. With especial venom guards *lived* to *fuck with* black, Latino, and queer cats. So, they systematically *fucked with* the people who taught and worked with black, Latino, and queer cats.

Whatever, we were there on the inside.

Very soon after Hatti's and Ahmed's desire got stoked on the inside— happily for them, Ahmed was paroled. Ahmed was a beautiful man. He was a brilliant man. Hatti was a beautiful woman—and a brilliant woman. And they loved one another, or so they thought they did. They were good together on the inside. Out of the joint, Ahmed could not stay away from the cause of his time inside in the first place—smack. Their relationship deteriorated to bits. The drug test and attempted robbery sent Ahmed back to the inside for a longer time, despite all the witnesses to his goodness and 'good' potential.

And outside, like many, Hatti and I went back to the brassiere.

ii. wayward ways

the last thing i said to him this morning was a hostile goodbye
when he slid out to the sidewalk and onto a stale danish
at next door's convenience spot.

watched him from my balcony hop side to side on his way
on his way, wayward as he was. the wayward ways
broke my heart:
the casual part of cheek.

Spring 2022

i. winter

—a wounded fowl
claw slammed in my window,
in rural, Republican upstate New York
and a lone camel sequestered
at a recreational
camp for boys, nuzzling a tractor,
dreaming john deere its only friend.

ii. shoulder

a murder of crows hovered
above a head-
less deer on a narrow shoulder.

iii. survival artists

refugees are artists
of survival, of unnamed
corpses, of mass graves
            and unmarked stones.

iv. catskills elegy: journal entry

last five miles of upstate drive dissolved in pink-orange late afternoon sun
bared of my soul bored of my mind two arresting beings appear: a beaute-
ous black brown stallion sporting its fierce rider in dark gear and shocks of
dark hair in time with the stallion's own holding reins closely and fully astride
unpredictability turning steed sharply south its gorgeous head and mane flat
to the wind onto our rural route and me heading north in late model sedan
turning half-circle sharply against the country traffic to track the haunting
riders.

Forsaken Elegies

i. Brother

Your gift was you could name any random
recording (and its personnel) on any random radio station
or record player.

You and I taxied downtown. Awkward silences
born of different fathers that rainy May evening: to celebrate
your twenty-sixth birthday and my fifteenth at the Howard Theatre.

Cannonball Adderley! Oscar Brown Jr.!
Best of all, sweet Nancy Wilson!

After the show you drag me backstage to seek her autograph.
As sweet Nancy smiles and inscribes my crumpled napkin,
she boldly checks you out fondling the neck
of your umbrella, standing next to me.

ii. Longing

Twenty or so years later on Cape Cod
I again spot Tisha dancing her feet off,
still pretty as high school, modishly *on-the-butch-side*,
making magical turns with a shorter, muscular black
woman, equally modish *on-the-butch-side*.
As a seventies anthem trails off I watch them walk out onto
the shabby pier, and the rest of the night through
surveil Tisha dancing and smiling into the eyes of and
tonguing her friend

so very deeply.

iii. out that door

away from me
on down that street
        switching
to some other doo-wop
in your arms
of imagi-
          nation
and you blow-
         ing some old
song: yeah yeah
        yeah-eh-eh-eh
oh, the surprise
and the same old
same ole
how can
        this be
        you'd ev-
        er leave
        me in
        some 'old
            leafy glade'
        to the intrusion of violins

and my old breaking heart
        needs to belong

at last
(oh i just want to die)

Make me a habit of you

was my invocation thirty-two years ago
when I cast all caution for your love

onto the Atlantic seacoast
(where four hundred years had already been cast)

not that you'd love me
that you'd let me love you

whether I stay or go
there's no love for nobody else

Too much to bear

body of Three Irons—
mother of six—

what must her children have thought
when she was brought
to their sad grandmother?

one child asks,
'did she hurt
long
in those cool mountains?'

'an eagle shot by a greedy hunter,'
sad grandmother explains.

many many bodies in these cool mountains.
many, many mothers daughters sisters aunties girlfriends
grandmothers missing dead
reduced
to exigencies
of extractive practices.

Uvalde, Texas, May 24, 2022

Dare I then poetize
the moment eleven-year-old
M. took and rubbed all over herself
the blood of one of her nineteen fallen classmates
and lay down next to her?
('Pretend to sleep, baby,' whispered the wise Charleston grandmother.)
Dare I versify how it was:
to witness their two teachers gunned down
(who might have at one time taught the assassin)
to be the first, tenth, or eighteenth fourth grader shot
by an anomalous automatic rifle-toting malcontent
(not that good a shot either,
except up close in tight space)?
For nearly an hour murder and mayhem
swift as early COVID.

'Shot his grandmother just before he mass-murdered two Texas classrooms,
    adjoined.
It always begins with misogyny,' opines a deft historian.

And police wait *not* to be afraid?

Mother Emanuel Nine: their influence was wide

                    Mother
Emanuel African Methodist
Episcopal Church Nine
Senior pastor state senator
Name meaning 'merciful'
Church eldress, oldest to be shot
Great grandnephew tries to shield her,
         the first and youngest shot
College administrator and pastor
         Doctor her last name not a title
Sunday school teacher
Track coach and pastor
Librarian
Church sexton
Seventy-four-year-old pastor

Two played dead

All women except two men

Shot while praying

And being black (and trusting).

Say their names:

Sharonda Coleman-Singleton, forty-five
Susie Jackson, eighty-seven
Myra Thompson, fifty-nine
Daniel Simmons, seventy-four
Ethel Lance, seventy
Cynthia Hurd, fifty-four

DePayne Middleton Doctor, forty-nine
Clementa Pinckney, forty-one
Tywanza Sanders, twenty-six

In one of the oldest black churches (older than the Confederate flag)

Denmark Vesey cofounder

Two hundred and three years old

Mother Emanuel
African
Methodist
Episcopal
Church
Nine

Remember Birmingham Sunday?

This horror unfolded on a Wednesday.

                    Mother Emmanuel
                            African
                    Methodist
                            Episcopal
                    Church
                            Nine

Say their names

Selected Poems

Believe me, putting together these thirty-nine years of poems has been quite the evocative experience. I found myself rather critical of the older work, wondering if I should include certain poems. But then that is why we call it "selected." I take a lesson from my sister poet, Audre Lorde, who had no problem revising years-old poems. So, "selected" assumes there will be revisions.

Included in this section are poems extending from my most recent publication, *Targets* (Bushel Editions, 2018), produced by my good friends of the Bushel Collective, a cultural organization in the Catskills, back to my beloved first book, *Narratives: poems in the tradition of black women* (Kitchen Table: Women of Color Press, 1982). There are poems chosen from *By My Precise Haircut* (Word Works, 2016), *The Days of Good Looks: The Prose and Poetry of Cheryl Clarke, 1980 to 2005* (Carroll and Graf, 2006), *Experimental Love* (Firebrand, 1993), *Humid Pitch* (Firebrand, 1989), and *Living as a Lesbian* (Firebrand, 1986).

Targets continues my study of black culture, opening with "History," which investigates life through various lenses, the meta, local, and intimate. Billie Holiday, for me the creator of modernism, is invoked throughout this poem, even when she's not the Billie the poem alludes to. "On Their Way to Life" hails two young people, Sandra Bland and Botham Jean, just starting out in life and cut down by racist rogue policemen.

I am deeply indebted to women's independent presses: Kitchen Table: Women of Color Press and its pioneering publishers, Cherríe Moraga and Barbara Smith; the equally pioneering Firebrand Books and its tireless publisher and editor, Nancy K. Bereano; and, most recently, the wonderful Word Works Books and its indefatigable editor and poet, Nancy White. My poems and essays have appeared in numerous lesbian, gay, and feminist publications over the years, but the anthologies to which I am most indebted are the lesbian feminist journal *Conditions*, which produced *Conditions Five, The Black Women's Issue* (1979); Cherríe Moraga's *This Bridge Called My Back: Writings by Radical Women of Color* (1981); Joan Larkin and Elly Bulkin's *Lesbian Poetry: An Anthology* (1981); and Barbara Smith's *Home Girls: A Black Feminist Anthology* (1983). These precious books set me on my writing journey and created loyal audiences who continue to support my work and that of many other lesbian writers.

I have drawn the "Selected Poems" from the volumes mentioned above. In looking back over four decades of published work, I can only say I count myself fortunate to have been in the lesbian community and to have had my poetry embraced by women of all backgrounds, colors, ethnicities, sexualities, and ages. Lesbian community, solidarity, and creativity have kept me going, and still do.

Targets

(2018)

History

Don't be so quick to bury your stars and bars
in some museum of military history.

i.

'When an incident occurs like the Michael Brown police murder, black
    people see history:
slavery, the betrayal of Reconstruction, Jim Crow, Plessy, Lynch Law,
    segregation,
(Mississippi Goddamn). Cops see only the one event,' says a venerable
    Southern historian.

(Cops see history too; the history of their racist rationalizations and that
    dark body lying and bleeding on an August street).

Both act accordingly.

Cops bring down the brutal force of the state upon us, black people—
    women and men. And we,
black people, see history.

ii. Billie Holiday

The answers are not in our stars, baby girl, why you got sucked down that
    drain. Your baby
voice and cool knowledge.
Why? You had everything in it.
If there was one story I had the power of prerogative to change—besides the
    2016 presidential election—yours is the one every time I hear you sing one
    of those droll
tunes you made art
and the legend
of your leg atop a shabby dressing room vanity trying to get a good vein.

iii.

President Obama takes to Twitter. His 'followers' tweet: 'WELCOME TO TWITTER, NIGGER.'

iv.

While I can casually dismiss having had an affair with a married (straight) woman, I will never forget Louise. Her long black hair whipped back into a ponytail like Billie's in the late fifties and a fabulous, extravagant sense of humor and love of cannabis that sent my inexperienced mind and me into an orbit of nonsense and theater that nearly ended or at least ruined my life. There I was on that fated morning left with the husband, Billy, downstairs shouting up at me:

'Tell Louise to come out of that apartment this minute or I'm going to break your door in.' And Billy did, and she ran out past him, stepping over shards of glass, to her Pontiac and leaving both of us there, staring after her.

Police no match for the tall elegance of gray suit and straight black man desperation to follow Louise, with .38 protruding hard against his front trouser pocket, handkerchief wrapped around the bleeding hand he had punched in the glass with. I admired his resistance—despite myself—for the way the pigs jumped back.

> 'Wait a minute, buddy,' they say weakly as they fall back onto the
> hood of their squad car.
> 'You wait, you cops. Don't you buddy me,'
> Billy snaps.

Cops later pronounced the event 'a tiff between the boyfriend and the girlfriend.' (Who is whom?)

v.

I can still recall that desire. Walking out onto my street to meet her as she leaves from her Pontiac, the seat of many
rendezvous.

We see each other a block away. Put-on laughter of recognition. Each moseying to the other, heads and hips cocked, the resonant certainty of our kinesis, drawing closer.

Fitted linen dress, bare legs, high heels—brief-less.
Boxer shorts, tank top, high-tops—bra-less.

On Their Way to Life

i. #Sandra Bland

A fly black girl brown skin and open brown face, anything but bland—even
in that mug shot and orange jumpsuit on your way to life by way of Prairie
   View, Texas,
now joining the long list of infamous sites
where unarmed black death thrives in cop custody
if you're changing lanes and smoking a cigarette at the same time
(but check it out: a fly black girl smoking a cigarette brown skin open brown
   face—
even when pissed
after telling you to dump your smoke brags
        'I'll light you up'
and drags you from your car
like lynching, except you were in custody—though not convinced
of its lawfulness:
        'You're gonna arrest me for changing a lane?'

ii. leaving Chicago

Mamie Till knew quite a bit about lynching. After crow-barring open that
coffin saw the telltale ring, and, as she claimed, felt over every inch of what
was left of Little Man's body, dredged up from Money, Mississippi. (Black
people get lynched over whistling selling cigarettes playing loud music
talking loud talking back praying running driving with defective taillights
playing with toy guns wearing hoodies and reaching for our own damned
wallets.)

Don't be black, coming from Chicago and traveling south you may not stand
the storm if you're a sassy black teenager whistling or a fly black girl smoking
and unused to taking low to nonsense—even fatal nonsense. Better to stay
with the extreme temperatures of your Midwest metropole than to cross the
median in a Texas prairie town or a Mississippi delta.

iii. #Botham Shem Jean from St. Lucia

Always good at math
on your way to life in Dallas, Texas
Botham Shem Jean.
Minding your own business.
In your own apartment your day's accounting work done.
A punk gun-happy off-duty cop white girl maybe drunk thinks you are in hers
bursts in on you
watching tv (*in your own apartment*)—and shoots you in the torso
before
she realizes
she's not in her apartment and
you aren't in her apartment either?

Targets

North Miami—or any part of Miami for that matter.
(Remember Liberty City, 1980, Arthur McDuffie?)
PD snipers finishing their target practice
on mug shots
—some as old as fifteen years—of black male subjects
when an unsuspecting upstanding clarinetist Sgt. of the Florida Army
  National Guard Band enters
with her fellow Guards-persons for 'weapons qualification
training'—amidst hulking white bodies bulked up with tats short-sleeve tees
  tight levis cowboy boots baseball football trucker caps
and—whaddaya know—hoodies—sees her brother's image amongst other
  targets
scored with bullets—complains poignantly of 'hits' in his head and eye,
declares: 'That's not his life, now. He's a father. He's a husband. He's a career
man. He works a nine-to-five.'

Open Heart Surgery

4/10:
Surgeon must be able to insert his hand into heart region.
Six hours under his hand, coronary bypass for another six.

The slight male night
nurse, youngish, maybe gay, white,
feels my hands, comments,
'Boy, your hands are cold,'
returns with two
folded tunnel-like
large white terry-cloth heated heaps
places them
on my lap, implores,
'Here, put your hands in these,'
I do.

Morning, asks permission
to give me a sponge bath,
changes bandage on chest incision
and dates with his Sharpie
'4/12.'

I think of him often.

depth in a two-dimensional space

for T. J.

background middle
fore
blur details: cooler colors
more detail: color more intense warm colors
complement next to complement to stand out
make grayer blue orange red green yellow purple cold far away warm close up
and the many shades of gray

assignment: still life in warm colors remember: more water than pigment

Brief Interval

I knew what I was about stroking
your lovely neck
perilously brief interval
intersection of desire
the real
and feminist derring-do.

Intersection is three or four points
of variance, divergence, diversion,
aversion, and hapless brief interval
larger than a grid
in dread of a walled corner
a piano stool, a contraband .38
and flip of an eye eros
oh throat.

I don't do well with expectation.
I need plot.
Come up here if it's too cool a story
below with your windows cracked.
Higher is warmer
in this last, fast phantasmic
interval.

Legacy/Legends

suspended in a trance trapeze like
blankness at the red light
slipping to sleep from this hell
the thousand slights, slings, and piercing
things the children endure post-Brown
due to fortunes of color.

The sneer of lips and snarl of larynx
fill my passenger window on this overcast hot afternoon—

    'Ain't you that integratin' nigger?'

while I lift the Colt from its place on the passenger seat,
and with a fool's certainty
aim it between the pores of his nostrils:

    'And—ain't you that segregatin' cracker I'm now 'bout to drop
      right heah?'

lipstick corny

for M. S.

lipstick
on wineglass corny
mark of femme-memory.
sage, basil, dill, parsley
harvested from planted pots
gifts to our worthless, reckless, feckless souls,
every one.

(cigarettes oh cigarettes
—never free of nicotine's je ne sais quoi—and reefer,
jamais assez,
when your dealer dies quietly quickly of cancer.)

then, spotting the wineglass take it up:
'i'll have wine now.'
'red?'

'there's also vouvray.'

'the malbec, its bright magenta rim.'
so much cover for eros,

and a next morning memory
ephemeral
lipstick on wineglass
corny
or a gift
against our dread of naming?

What does it mean?

to be five years old and kill your family pet?
Probably you will enjoy murder mysteries
as an adult. Possibly you will write them.
Undoubtedly you will have empathy for the murderer
remembering the sensation of grabbing
that random butcher knife from the table
confining puppy to a corner and stabbing her
through the middle with a quick underhand jab
and your delight in puppy's alien scream causing
mother to race to the scene fearing the wild cry
herself screaming pushing you out of her way
as she tries to stanch the wound with dishtowels
wiping the floor simultaneously and yells
at you to get the hell out of her sight,
'before
I stab you.'

Forty-Eight Years

King'd come into Birmingham or Albany or Selma or Chicago or Memphis in
  two ways:

Way One,
according to witness: during the day and with him come the
paparazzi and the front-page Pulitzer winners,
and then in three days King'd leave—and
leave the clean-up
to the foot
soldiers.

Way Two,
according to legend: by evening with his crowd
of preachers after plates of smothered short ribs mac and
cheese collards
candied sweets King'd say to his confreres
(despite endless self-recrimination): 'Time to
go souling.'

Woman Ends Her Life: Elegy

'To those who have wanted to see my body buried
can now have the opportunity.'

Found last Monday by one of her neighbors hanging
by the neck dead in her house
judging from the condition of the body
had been there several days
as she had not put in an appearance
neighbors investigated and found her as stated:
leaving the above epitaph hanging by the neck
judging from the condition of the body
there several days.

Rather eccentric
known at times to disappear
without saying where when or how long
there several days judging from the condition of
the body.

Tercet

The Confederate flag:
Don't be so quick to bury your stars and bars
In some museum of military history.

Reckless Domesticity

I am a reckless locked door.
Can't be kept from jumping
out a window. Runaway six
months. Justus hid me in
his master's carriage house
ten miles down the road.

I felt good. When the patrollers caught
me and brought me back, Miss Zen
beat me hard but not hard enough
to keep me from running again.

Running until I run far enough
to stay free. Free is a worrisome thing
to get even when you get there.

And get there can I live in it?

Living as a lesbian in the archive of style

I remember one summer I worked a lot in Washington Square Park. It must have
been about 1966. The park was divided. It has these walks, sort of like a sunburst,
and there were these territories staked out. There were young hippie junkies down one
row. There were lesbians down another, really tough amazingly hard-core lesbians.

—DIANE ARBUS IN *DIANE ARBUS*, 1972

Short-sleeve banlon pullover,
gabardine pleated slacks,
silk socks, and the smallest size wing-tips?
—this what you mean by 'hardcore'?

Or *Regular* Lucky Strike pack rolled up into the sleeve of a white white
and very pressed tee inside black black chinos, highly polished black penny
loafers, and Clorox white crew socks—this 'hardcore'?

Or conked and coifed à la Jackie Wilson or Dee Clark?
Or quiffed and pomped à la Elvis or Tony Curtis? 'Hardcore'?

Or lastly by 'hardcore,' do you mean
steadfast in the practice of waiting for
and on their femmes, more schooled
in subtleties, who rescued their butches
and raised them the rest of the way,
while nasally singing,

> *Come on ovah heah, daddy.*
> *Let me throw my long legs*
> *round yo' perfect neck*

> *and rockya rockya rockya a little while*

Juanita

for Derrais Carter, archivist

I can't wait
and get up from here and find my drawers and shoes
and plait my hair (back up)
every time having to take it a-loose and lie down and pose up on my arm and
    do as
he say in front of that box. If only
all I have to do is take
my plaits a-loose

By My Precise Haircut

(2016)

Mandela: 12-5-2013

i.

Detroit journalist Marc Crawford introduced me to 'Nelson'
from a stack of circa 1970 Pathfinder Press pamphlets of his
pre-prison speeches in those days of intense indie publishing.

Then, pointing to an oval-shaped, mahogany-colored three-foot object
with sprouts of white and dark hair—surely something's
hide—suspended on the back of his bathroom door, then
hefting the encumbrance to his shoulder, and then, like a comic
mimicking fucking thrusting it forward at me, Marc swore:

> 'I will be there with it when he gets free.
> This is his shield. He is Xhosa, you know.
> He gave it to me. Before Rivonia. To keep.
> I told him at his sentencing I would give it back
> to him when he's released.'

ii.

I read that pamphlet and memorized
Mandela's pie-shaped face,
off-center part in African hair,
and tribal leopard-skin cape
slung over his naked chest.

iii.

After the fall of Motown, wiry Willie Kgositsile
shouted through his broadsides,

'They used to call it Detroit!'

And that was forty years ago.
And that was yesterday.

a capital car chase

in memory of Miriam Carey, 1979–2013

Ah, if you would condone drone strikes
you would condone surveilling me here in little old
Stamford, Connecticut.

You finally got the starch to stand up to those Negro-hating
Republicans.

All those (white) patients I had to clean daily spying on me
through their implantology and root canals.

How weary I became looking in their mouths, especially
if they asked what kind of
degree I have—code for was I was qualified enough to be looking down
their fetid throats—and 'who takes care of your daughter while
you work?' and 'what does your husband do?'

All that would be enough to send anybody careening onto
1600 Pennsylvania Avenue in a late model Infiniti. No car
lasts forever. But my daughter survived in that luxury-car
baby carseat, poor little orphan. New York child services says
she's fine, though. Imagine how my family will have to spin
my 'wrongful death' to her.

Ah, I shall not speculate on the obvious.

I drove to 1600 Pennsylvania Avenue, unarmed, because I
heard his droning voice telling me he couldn't do anything
about the voices luring me to Federal Triangle that day.

Why, he even monitored my funeral.

'Did they really have to shoot her to death? Hunh? Just post-
partum depression with a little psychosis,' *chirps my tearful
sister.*

*(Couldn't none of you all speak up before? Break the
silence? Why do black people always have to be at the proverbial
end of a frayed rope before anyone declares,
'You are crazy.')*

*Ah, how that ammo hurt—but not for long.
Ah, and how invisible I still was to the Hill that never
noticed my demise.*

'Did I have to lose a sister?'

You still asking that, Sis?

'Couldn't they have shot her tires?'

Are you kidding, Sis? Cops can't shoot that straight.

'She was unarmed,' *Mama cries.*

*They had to aim for the overkill, Mama. Remember that one hundred forty-five
    pound African?
Forty-one shots later and all he had was a billfold.*

Women of Letters

i. Belinda's Petition Remembered

I was stolen.

Seventy years toiling this side of the sea, verdant
forests, mountains, seasons of color, heat, and the ruthless cold.
Odd creatures. Never a moment to myself, honorable
sirs. We are suing. Seventy years and am I not less than a slave
that I cannot protect myself from the betrayal of abandonment
by who called himself my master, a loyalist fleeing, leaving me
and my infirm daughter to dwell in penury? We are suing.

(You, sirs, perhaps may imagine the rigors of that voyage.
Three hundred Africans. I lay above deck between two women not of my
language chained to one another by the ankles. Our doom
slavery. We were separated in Tobago. A young girl made to lay
me between her nubile breasts to Virginia but was not able to
fight off the abominators, escaping overboard their hairs and
smells.)

We are suing.

ii. PLEASE READ

Pulaski, Tennessee, July 15, 1883

DEAR FRIENDS:

I am trying to find out where my children are. Please help me. Their names are Diana, Henry, Drucilla and George Washington. Before the war we belonged to Mr. W. M. Thompson, in Rutherford County, North Carolina. About thirty years ago, after the death of our old Mistress, Diana and Drucilla were taken from me and carried into Georgia. George Washington was taken away from Jackson County, Alabama, by the soldiers during the war.

I, their mother, was Hannah Thompson, but have since married a man named Powers. Please read this notice in the churches, and any one knowing of my children will confer a favor by writing to me.

Address,
HANNAH POWERS,
  Pulaski, Tennessee.

iii. Letter from a close friend written four days after you die and received three days after your birthday

April 22, 1967
905 4 Ave So Apt 1
Great Fall Mont
738 Madison St. N. W.
Washington, DC

Hi Hannah.

Just a few lines to let you here from me the reason I am so long writing you is because I have had the flue again and still can't shake it off I still have it but not as bad as at first I just ant felt like writing or doeing nothing Just do fix my food when I get like this it leave me weak and the days is so so long out here. And the nights to I have a lot of friends but still get lonesome here for home so I will try to get home in July if I dont have no more sickness but I have spent a lot of money for sickness. So I will trust in God and he will help me. I eat just what I wont and any time I think about cornbread and greens I think about you and cooking chitlings for Friday and Sat. if the Lord spears me. I have sent Bertha cards and a letter and she still don't write so I ant going to write her no more. Do Mildred still live where she did and what have become of Marion and May and Anna Perry. I sure hope all that old bunch will be living when I get home it is snowing like mad now will write more next time and wont be so long answering.

Give all your family my love.

From a friend
Geraldine

All ways glad to here from you.

oh memory fateful and fatal

i. elegy for 1963

how many anniversaries can anyone accommodate in one year not
to live in anticipation of events to become next year's celebrations
and memorializations?

Jackson, Mississippi: 'NAACP Field Secretary Medgar Evers Shot' in
the back getting out of his car in front of his house and strong man
that he is, drags himself up by his car door handle, staggers up the
steps, collapses on his front porch as Mrs. Evers, the three little
Evers, and awakened neighbors look on hysterically, one fires a shot
to scare off the assassin.

Washington, DC: our neighbor, recent widow Mrs. Flowers, joins us
full of hope as we ride the bus to the Lincoln Memorial on that hot
August day for 'Jobs and Freedom,' returning
to watch 'I Have a Dream' on television. Tipped off by FBI,
Maryland State Police turn back Klansmen just outside the
District line, carful of weapons.

Birmingham, Alabama: when Mrs. Davis, a neighbor, drives a
frantic Mrs. Robertson to the 16th Street Baptist Church
where the dynamite detonated into the basement choir practice, Mrs.
Robertson's father breaks the news of her daughter Carole's murder,
'She's gone, baby.'

Dallas, Texas: asked by an aide if she would like to 'clean up' from the
blood, Mrs. Kennedy advises, 'Let them see what they have done.'

ii. zapruder

i google-hunt that zapruder film on youtube enhanced with color and
slow-mo and pant for the frames where jack thinking to smooth his
hair back from his face instead surprised grips his hand over his
forehead and the other over his throat as the first bullet enters and
exits his neck and turning to jackie falls over on her shoulder as the
second shot tears into that cool hyannis-bred brain and jackie in her
white kid gloves chases that brahmin brain as it is jettisoned out onto
the deck of that sleek '61 lincoln before the secret service forces her
back by jack's fallen side while the rest of us take cover in front of
screens and on the lawn across the street from that texas schoolbook
depository and wonder if a third or fourth shot was fired and all
those years we thought jackie was trying to escape out the back of
that fully-loaded presidential continental for as she told her maid the
next day 'i thought they might've killed me too.'

a sister's lament as she poses for an AP photograph holding her dead sister's portrait

Black women are accustomed to being firsts, and here you go
being first again:

Sgt. J. L. Winters,

'first [African] American [u.s.]/[black] servicewoman [of
mixed ancestry] to die since the war [against/with
Afghanistan] began.'

Says Ron, our family friend:
'The price we have to pay for what happened on 9/11.'

Why? Is your body to be bartered, levied, or charged?
Does he not know it was priceless and peerless and that you knew
what you were stepping to?

And here I stand
for the public
holding this picture of you in your uniform
(looking so pretty in it)
and your eyes aren't convinced
or resigned
to being 'the price.'
Nor are mine.

We look eerily identical
but opposite.
I'm dressed in jeans, tee shirt, and parka.
I don't half-smile or look into the camera with old glory
displayed behind me.

I fairly suck my teeth and stare piss-faced
askance with a suburban chimney as backdrop.

I look like a ventriloquist
holding this portrait instead of you in my arms.

I'm lonely as a convict out here outside of Gary
while you are crashed into a mountainside in Pakistan.

A mysterious mistake.
Not 'hostile fire,' say the secretaries
and generals.
Were you thinking it'd end this soon?
We look eerily identical.

songs of longing

for Sandra Rattley of Washington, DC

i. rainbow at the Regal '65

There's   a   rainbow
i-in my heart   tha-at
reminds me-ee of
of how we pa-ar-ted . . . .
My love is gone forever.
But deep down in my heart,
I'll love her forever . . . .

Screeching screams of fantasy seekers
vying with the precise insistence of a favorite falsetto.

> *Whatever   it   is   the rainbow*
> *is never enough*
> *even when the suicide is*
> *so well-planned.*
> *The superintendent reads from your note who to contact*
> *to take the body down*
> *and damn you for tying that slip knot so expertly*

High-pitched swoons.
Homage at the Regal.
One mo' chance.
Lonely duke, duke, duke, duke
of Chicago.

Oh Chi'.

ii. South East (S.E.)

Like Marvin
I used to be too nervous
to party.
We're from the
same town
but he grew up
in South East
a shantytown
of jacklegs like his father ('Father')
who, after making him strip naked,
beat the boy Marvin
almost every day
and almost forty years later shot
Marvin in a coke rage,
Marvin, that is.
'C'était tragique'
a Parisian tabloid quotes
a Motown spokesperson
in LA.

That's what we still think about
that rough trash in South East (S.E.).
Not like us farther *in* in North East (N.E.)
more than a decade later in our
segregated developments beginning
that long lateral stride into North West (N.W.)
and the lower middle class.

iii. 2007

for the big o
loving you forty years late
loving mucus stockpiling in your throat
loving that relentless climax
who will sing to us since your passion died?
who will sing passion to us?
who will sing passion?

iv. ice man

Broken up blues hymn
between my synapses:
deeper and wider than any
sho nuff sea

Broken up blues hymn
panting
crying against the wall of frequency
wanting

Broken up blues hymn
twanging signals
VeeJay amp   velvet larynx
satin tux   patent pumps

Broken up blues hymn muted grief
uncertain of
what tomorrow brings

'Don't try to spare my feelings.
Just tell me that we're through.'

v. falsetto

if r&b songs of unrequited love are channeling ex-slaves'
sadness hurt disappointment and pissed hostility at white
people's dastardly treatment of them and everybody else's
asses darker than a whiter shade of pale but especially
black asses;
then the tight pants patent loafers green-eyed
hair laid all the way to sunday morning miracle
falsetto boy was the deepest exponent of
ooh, ooh, ooh
oh, oh, oh
woo, hoo, ooh
baby baby.

vi. coda

parlor dance party with an ipod of five thousand songs only as far
back as charles brown. sandy my oldest friend a good dancer
since junior high school to come bop with me and pony
across some linoleum or hardwood & long for my mother
(who surveilled me slow drag with a mustachioed boy named
james a caramel baritone year older—and shy). yes,
do that party and reprise those gritty songs that fed and
desegregated the soul. yes, do it with some rhythm. more so
some substances. all those dumped cadavers. yeah. all that
studio work and live shows and riots. and y'all dead. hey,
y'all dead, comin' home. back in my (project) arms again.
heroin. cancer. and grits. a party like grits. yeah. come and
git it. left sitting on the dock and rock was reprising what we
knew already. gimme that baby sound falsetto aching tenor
that passion and phlegm: *shame on me shame on me I made*
a big mistake when I see my babe again I'ma bake me a
cherry cake ten thousand dollar reward for the first one who find
her when I git my hands on her I'm gonna just chain and bind
her. a need-tuh-need-yuh-baby sound to dance party to.

like the 45 the cd is over no matter the extra takes and still
yearning for when dancing was the life the stomp slop cha
cha cha tighten up the steps and turns and holding and
cradling arms and longing on linoleum and hardwood 'til
school or mule intervention.

The empire

you built, Ruth,
on that red and black label
           spin
     ning
           round that
skinny spindle of rhythm and
commerce for Ertegun,
the Mardins,
and Wexler.

Twenty-five years later:
making your comeback
wanting to listen to your
old 'stuff,'
discovering 'So Long' on 78
dust jacket intact
one hundred dollars
in an LA record shop
got you really pissed over those sixty-nine-dollar royalty
checks for the music you made.

Inventress of the hoochie
coochie. Whacking that tambourine on your
right crinoline backside. Fanning your own lovely bosom.
Making white mothers wanna
keep their sons at home
and white fathers wanna treat
their daughters mean.

a child die

for Amina Baraka

i. Shani Baraka and Rayshon Holmes

I went to that courtroom in New Jersey to see Ibn Pasha,
domestic abuser and killer of 'hard-loving black women,'
Shani Baraka and Rayshon Holmes, Shani's 'companion.'
Ibn Pasha estranged mate of Shani's older sister. Skinny, nerdy, color
of a walnut shell, innocuous-looking in Buddy Holly frames.
Killer.

So unlike the stern, serious revolutionaries Sundiata Acoli
and Assata Shakur in that same courtroom where I surveilled
injustice and the unjust daily thirty-eight years ago.

After sneaking back to the house to further harm his wife,
instead, Ibn Pasha shoots Shani and Rayshon in the head and body
multiple times. Steals Shani's watch, gift from 'Ray,' pawns it
in Baltimore.

Twenty-eight years ago I wrote a baleful poem to Shani's aunt—Kimako
Baraka/Sondra Elaine Jones—a 'hard-loving' (woman-
loving) black woman too, also murdered by a misguided man
who also stole her jewelry. Put up so tough a fight, he had to
stab her in the head and body multiple times.

Reticent naming is not witness enough.

ii. Kyra Mills

posted with photo on a mailbox at 14th St. and 6th Ave., New York City, fall 2001

six years old

last seen hold-

ing her mother's hand
on the ninety-second floor of Tower One.

iii. à Jacqueline

(Haiti, January 30, 2010)

Jacqueline, ten years old, sunk ten feet under five feet of concrete, her
classmate lying near. Chris, her rescuer and a missionary
from the States, only had a hammer. He needed help.
Jacqueline had been praying for hours—for herself, her
classmate lying near, and for Chris. So had Chris. He knew
the classmate was dead. He stopped digging as afternoon
gave way to twilight.

> 'I will be back. I must get help. It is getting dark. I need light and help
> and more tools. I will be back. Pray. Pray.'

Walk four miles to a bus.

> 'Four hours to get to my house.'

Drive back in the morning.

> 'Race to where I had last held her prayers in
> my ears, to the cinder block and concrete
> burial ground the school had become.'

Jacqueline was dead.

> 'How could a child die?
> Would she have held on if she knew I would be back in the
> morning. I mean, if I had said it. If I had said,
> *I will be back in the morning.*
> This will haunt me for more than a while.'

iv. Sakia
(1987–2003)

Hey, girl, I want you to know.
I'm gonna miss you so much if you go.

Thought your 'AG' truth could stop that reckless mouth
battering us all our black woman lives? He is in jail for twenty-five years
with the specter of that knife he stabbed into your fearless
fifteen- almost sixteen-year-old breast one early mo/urning at
Broad and Market in Newark, NJ.

Let us mark
the bloody space of your martyrdom
your no-place-to-be-who-you-were.

Our collusion.

v. a brave puppeteer

If not a brave puppeteer and member of the drama club a good soloist
a behind the scenes class president twice and your whole future before
you—we might not have known about this horror in Milford, CT., where
they think it's another world and safe for children but it's not—like,
remember Sandy Hook? Same old world of white male presumptuous
and privileged desire: dark depressed tuned-out turned down and needing
reassurance. And surely a girl with the last name Sanchez should want to
reassure him, a friend since middle school.

Stabbed you in the neck. In the hallway of John Law High School—
'Law'? This won't be a sonnet. Bled to death in front of teachers librarians
staff in the math wing where they think it's another world and safe for
children but it's not—like, Sandy Hook—the same old world of white male
presumptuous and privileged desire: dark depressed tuned-out turned down
and needing reassurance in front of teachers librarians and staff.

A friend since middle school. This won't be a sonnet.

How safe she thought she'd be when she left out that early morning.

A brave puppeteer.

The Days of Good Looks: 2000–2005

(2006)

living as a lesbian underground, fin de siècle

here under this pile of twentieth century,
my ass is sore from
taking in air on the underside of this mask.
so close i have worn it since the defoliation
of 14th street.
a high blown and wasted blues.
the same vamp after sorry vamp.
and burning indochine flesh.

Billie Holiday

mostly was thinking
about singing the song
once she got to carnegie,
columbia,
or café society
not
some fbi john back at
the attucks or the grampian
taping opium to the back of the commode
and stealing her money.
it's an intellectual process and
'in-dee-pendent-lee bloo-oo-oo.'
calculating future
to tell the story this time
never the same way twice.
sung or heard
so many times the same story
but bent or slant
so constant and so uncertain.
the perfect tongue-in-cheek of
'to whomever you love.'
the empress pops prez.
a lost-wax process.

Dreams of South Africa

i. Geography, 1958

Representing South African apartheid to Catholic grade-school children, in a secondhand geography textbook, a photograph of a line of *black* black men, shirtless, frowning, sitting down from the drudgery of whatever menial work they'd been allowed to do for the day. Racist middle-school captions scribbled by previous users under each man: 'your boyfriend,' 'liver lips,' 'blackie,' 'n——.'

ii. Progeny, 1966

I was an aspiring petite bourgeoise in my second year of college when the Unilateral Declaration of Independence occurred in Rhodesia, now Zimbabwe. Ian Smith, Rhodesia's president/dictator has the same name as a Hollywood Brit who played King Arthur among other guy roles in the 1930s. The progeny of Cecil Rhodes has a lot to answer for.

iii. Rutgers, 1977–1985

Eight years culminated in a thirty-day strike that lent itself easily to poetry. 'Divest,' the students told us. I was on their side though passing on both. I unloaded gallons of spring water from my station wagon every night at the site of the takeover. Behind a desk 8:30 to 4:30.

I read poetry one night, rousing to cheers a sleepy crowd of 'township' members after the first 15 days and nights camped on the commons, which they renamed 'Biko Township.' The aim of poetry: to silence obligatory clapping. Some Brit chick before me plodded self-righteously through a lecture on the plight of South African women—black and white. She commended me for my poetry: 'You even stirred this crowd.' She was an empirical chick and clearly skeptical of poetry.

iv. Tutu's daughter, 1988

I had a really serious auto accident the day I was to meet Desmond Tutu's daughter. Sideswiped on the left front by a tractor-trailer. (The damage was such an eyesore that my close friend, an agnostic, grabbed me and thanked God I was alive.) Bishop Tutu's daughter rode graciously to and from the campus in that car.

I asked after her father:

'He's behaving himself,' she said, grimly smiling.

She damned apartheid eloquently and liked to smoke cigarettes after. She defined family under apartheid as dedicated to its overthrow.

v. The two, 1989

were actors. One played a father whose daughter dies in the revolution. The other played his neighbor, an informer who redeems himself. I drove them to Manhattan that night after their intimate two-man performance. They would return to Johannesburg before the week was out.

They were brown happy-talking men like the jaunty porcupine
before she gives up her quills.

One fortyish, the playwright; the other sixtyish and handsome.

Both bore deep facial scars and keloid lesions.

Marks of apartheid—a drawer slammed shut on your sister's naked nipple.

To have a theater. To speak another truth. They'd made many journeys alone and together, any one could have meant certain death. Despite this they were happy-talking men and brown.

'Is Fugard the only South African playwright you people produce here?' the fortyish brother called cheerily back to me from the train track after our warm goodbyes.

vi. Manhattan, 1990

I was to do a reading somewhere in Manhattan. On the program as well, a member of the ANC talking on the economics of apartheid, how blacks fared, and how we in 'the West' could continue our resistance.

He was a stocky, tight, brown spring, grossly preoccupied, breathing audibly—what Fanon would call 'combat breath'—and young not so young as Tutu's daughter, but still younger than forty. Smoking heavily. Kind.

vii. KwaZulu-Natal, 2001

Having spent seventeen long, wide, and tight days in the province of KwaZulu-Natal very close to the ground, the fevered pitch of resistance can be heard and the lost bones of children touched. Back in Jersey City, an industrial burg across from Manhattan on the Hudson, I accept the loss of the Twin Towers on this frighteningly beautiful day. I watch askance from the car on the Newark Bay Extension the Second Tower implode behind me and disintegrate in the space between my right shoulder and earlobe.

james dean longing

during a hard nod one night in 1972: intruder jerome johnson, red-eyed and
   aspiring to film, sibilant, from his hot director's chair, declaims:

   'jimmy was the first fesminist!' (confusing 'feminist' with 'faggot,' I think
      baldwin)

later that year jerome johnson gunned down in columbus circle is framed
   for the evening news butt facing the camera the body of a famous mafioso
   on him

his brooch with cameo portrait of jimmy snatched purposefully from his
   chest by one of the assassins.

inside the brooch: james dean longing his scowl and protean lips tucked and
   disheveled white trash and preppie bloody drunk

(sal natalie rock pose for sex just beyond the take)

Experimental Love

(1993)

War Crazy Men

We are everywhere and white people still do not see us.
They force us from sidewalks.
Mistake us for men,
Expect us to give up our seats to them on the bus.
Challenge us with their faces.
Are afraid of us in groups.
Thus the brutal one-on-one.
Like a TV news script, every transaction frustrates rage.
Hand in hand with me
you admonish
not to let them come between us
not to let them come between us on the street.
We are struck by war crazy men
recording their gunfire on stereo cassette decks.

Greta Garbo

Easter Sunday, April 15, 1990

I imagine you left Hollywood at thirty-six
because you had enough money to live as a lesbian
and didn't have to buy into heterosexuality
after Christina.

I imagine you overlooking the East River
or in Saks in fur coat
and sensible shoes asking,
'Please, do you have men's pajamas?'
I imagine a life of guarded anonymity, autonomy, alcoholism
all over Switzerland, the French Riviera,
and Italy wearing pants, flats, floppy hats,
dark glasses, and
toasting whiskey with an Alsace baroness
who liked it up the ass
yearly on the Rhine.

Movement

I was a brown ball of a chap
when a small light-skinned Negro working woman
refused to give up her seat to a white bus rider.
Three months after, my father took me to our new church.
Surveying from a distance, I said, 'How pretty,'
to those pastel dots of white people.
My father warned, 'Hush, girl.'
I'd been taught the *Baltimore Catechism*
by cinnamon-faced oblates of Saint Thomas the Moor.
This would be my first mission.

ii.

His first mission Alabama.
The cotton bolls sway in the gentle dusk breeze.
Soft is the welcome darkening.
The evening star signals a tenuous freedom and workers
sing toward the Wednesday prayer meeting,
eager for the spirits.
A woman with one breast and thick plaits is overcome
by the refrain, *Walk, children, don't you get weary.*

iii.

Walk, children, and don't get weary
before you get to Mississippi.
It was rough. Mississippi.
People got killed
and maimed regular.
We learned to drive fast at night.
One night not fast enough.

Three of us.
Driver didn't die though shot in the neck.
The two of us got him to a hospital
and sent a telegram to the president.

iv.

The president never understood the Civil War.
That year I played alone at recess.
Boys on one side of the yard.
Girls on the other.
A nun at either end.
The boys' nun was five feet tall,
solid, and swarthy.
She spun like a top on her
thick black heels
when the boys tugged at her veil.
She was aloof from them though. And stern.
We surveilled one another the whole hour.

The girls' nun was giraffe-like
and levitated her brown lashes
in blue-eyed laughter
at girls gathering around her
for a touch, a word, a favor.
Her eyes sought mine every day
above their heads of flowing hair
always just before the bell rang.

v.

Just before the bell signaling the almsgiving,
handkerchiefs signaling anticipation,
he was overcome
by the burden of the love
people gave back to him.
He spoke from a familiar text that extraordinary night,
the joy of victory.

Finally, he fell back from the pulpit
full with it
into the arms of his angel.

vi.

No guardian angel could protect
this light-skinned black boy
in our school that had the last name Nixon.
His light-skinned black father, my dentist,
was voting for Nixon the first time
DC voted for a president.
The nuns pushed Democrats.
Kennedy called Coretta King
and every Negro in DC voted for him,
except Nixon's father.

vii.

Nixon's father was Edna Dockings's dentist, too. Edna Dockings was
our piano teacher. A birdish woman with bony, veiny, rubbery fingers
from years of abusive practice. Mrs. Dockings was full of uplift stories,
a graduate of Oberlin, and a Yankee. While she drilled us in her basement
studio on Schirmer's Library, she read us her grandmother's letter
from a great-aunt who drove off slave catchers regularly with stones.
She called all three of us 'Baby Sister.'

Mr. Dockings, 'Daddy,' practiced a monotonous cello from the third
floor and smoked a dirty pipe. He called Mrs. Dockings 'Edgy.' While
my two sisters received their lessons in the basement, I was made to
practice exercises on the faulty but sumptuous grand upstairs. Daddy
would stop his practice, come down, and ask me to play Mozart.

viii.

Ask me to play Mozart and
imagine me being beaten in my face by a white man
because I used a restroom

somewhere in Mississippi:
a black man is made to beat you until he tires
a white man beats you some more.
You laying on your stomach,
trying to keep your dress down,
screaming.
The white man whispering close to your ear,
'Black bitch, big ass, you better shet up and be still.'

ix. The Interview

'Even on Sunday slaves didn't deserve rest, sir.'
Rather unworthy, slaves. Not adequate. No real powers of discernment.
    No souls.

'A slave could be sick her water breaking feeble-minded or six years old,
    yet made to do unrelenting hard work any time night or day, sir.'

'Though I was never treated cruelly,
I saw dastardly deeds done to others
for the slightest lack of measure.
Strapped to a tree and get
a hundred lashes and then be washed with brine;
or made to drink a strong medicine, put in stocks,
foul on himself, and be left there for up to two days.
I saw a woman once. She cooked in the house.
Her mouth was locked with an iron muzzle.'

passing

i'll pass as a man today and take up public space with my urges in the casual
way he does in three-piece suit and gucci pumps big pants and large sneakers
tight jeans and steel-tipped boots read my newspapers spread-eagled across
a whole row of seats make my briefcase-boombox-backpack into an ottoman
on the seat across from me on the l.i.r.r.; and spread my legs from here to far
rockaway on the mighty i.n.d.; and when i get sleepy or bored spreading the
brim of my blue fedora on the bus to queens hunch down cross my fat feet
into the aisle or lean forward with my arms folded into the great press of
rush hour flesh:
hawking, spitting, and pissing all the way.

All Souls' Day

And we are in a bad way, directions uncertain.
How would we see the souls?
Afraid of each other but wanting our deaths,
and war threatening in some far-off bedroom.

This catacomb is a carnival of survival marvels
and language and no unhampered passage.
Their costumes tattered
matted hair
funny shoes
dirty legs
masks of tabloids and brown paper bags.
We embrace them in our anger at each other.
They are sucked back into the tunnel.
Half-masked we skip out onto the street
laughing at our little triumph
pretending we have no history
no sordidness
no deaths
and maiming
have never known the baby
who got a block of wood
forced in her tiny mouth for crying.

Flowers of Puerto Rico

Last night my table was adorned with roses,
although I did not get one cent for my lecture.

—FRANCES E. W. HARPER (1878)

i. Cruz de Martha

What or who is Martha's cross?
Lazarus sealed in a tomb but not dead?
The daily sorrow of her sister Mary?
Jesus's heat and desperation to roll back the stone?
('Behold how he loved him,' whispered the gossips.)
The putrid smell of a recent corpse?
Her own longing for the body?

Indians, impressed by the miracle of Martha's longing, named
the yellow, red, and pink blossoms Cruz de Martha to mark their
survival of the Resurrection.

ii. Reina de las Flores

Draping trees with purple,
you are the robe of Iphigenia,
whose father was signified to death
by that color for his murderous hubris,
Reina de las Flores.

The reckless Clytemnestra
drapes the purple robe over Agamemnon,
bloated from conquest.
How could she sleep with him
even out of duty
after such treacherous sacrifice
to appease the absent winds of Aulis?
After her own pact with Eros?

She prayed for the return,
and cultivated the moment,
gave herself up to its final paradox.

'She was my daughter. Her death was my death,'

said the queen as the knife drew closer.
Reina de las Flores,
the robe of Iphigenia,
the lies of mothers.

iii. Flamboyan

Bold flamboyan, flashing, flashing:
spray of passion,
beads of blood from the rose thorns,
or a rare refraction
of the sun?

Buttons

I wanted to unbutton every piece of your clothing
which was all buttons
from that silk shirt
down to the crotch of that gabardine skirt.
My buttons too:
my jeans brass-button up,
my shirt has six shell buttons,
my camisole has three tiny ones.
This restaurant is in my way
when I want to be unbuttoning
and unbuttoned.
Can't you tell?
To do it now.
To reach across the bread.
To start unbuttoning.
My arms so long.
My fingers faster than the eye and omnidextrous.
Now, ain't that loving you?

An Epitaph

(1902–1989)

Of Mabel Hampton. Pride.
Heritage. Girlfriend. Butch.
At the top of her Bronx stairs
frying fish.

Riding the running board
of an antique Ford
on Pride Day.

Years of ancient Pride:
      Runaway.
      Hoofer.
      the lucky bus stop.
Perpetual shrine to forty years.

Of Mabel Hampton in audiences of women
peering through dark lenses.
Soulmate.
Peerless.

Rondeau

They are bodies left unburied.
Instead of roaming the underworld, they've tarried
to bring their nomadic anxiety
to my world with little propriety.
I'd rather them waylaid in Staten Island, unferried.

Sit next to this one here, pass her, there's that one there.
This one's pretty, that one tall.
Her there, she's fair.
Haunt my solitude, hurt my silence, make me crazy.
They are bodies.

I try to act modern, but still I'm worried
We sleep together every night and still I'm worried
that she or she loves you more expertly sexually
than me obsessed by her or her like voices of insanity.
Provocative and sexy nonmonogamy in theory.
But they are bodies.

Makeup

i.

If I were to paint myself for you,
like a Nubian man, I'd paint my skin.
I'd do it at dusk by a bright fire.

Like a Nubian man, I'd squat,
genitals revealed and flaccid:

First the henna.
Then the ochre.
Then the ash.
Your breathing would quicken.

ii.

Mornings Mother painted herself.
Seated before her vanity applying powder and rouge.
For the exact applications of mascara and eyebrow pencil,
she'd stand leaning into her reflection.
Makeup was her art
like the Nubian.
Evenings she spent before her canvas.
She had passions and obsessions, my mother
with ledgers, loose leaf,
and peacock blue ink staining her fingers
from the day's cadenced relentless extractions.

Let her tattoo the dream of a perfect design
the dream of sunrays.
Let her make it a perfect cicatrix.

I watch her with the needle.
You are brave as the ink takes hold,
as the blood comes to the surface.
The sun is belligerent.

Remember the Voyage

for Noel Da Costa, 1929–2002

Remember the voyage
the leaving, the theft of mangoes
the poorly tuned but graceful fiddle
haunting Harlem school days
the small parlor.

Remember the breadfruit and ancient market women
marking their places,
gapped-tooth women of the calabash,
busy even after purple dusk cooled equatorial sun.
Remember mountains singing in the Caribbean,
and blue twilight of Harlem melting into bawdy moon.
The blood.
Remember the Etruscan ruin
and fingers seasoning unplucked strings.
Remember the calabash.

Arroyo

I am not a mountain to stand for millennia
to stare at nakedness
and be naked too.
I was very north
and you asked me to go farther.
I prefer the arroyo,
to receive the floods
that sometimes drown,
to be taken south.

Querida

Why take so long to ask for it?
Come on, kid, are you gonna go after it?
Two days.
I'm only here for four.
Must you be courted so?
Your lovely breasts want
to linger over me.
It's pouring out of you.
I called you weeks ahead
so you could free yourself up.

You bragged that you'd risk the taste
of a stranger's juices,
so committed to desire's destination,
your mouth, the flow of menses.
But you won't take the first step with me.
I have to undress you, undress myself,
pull down the bedclothes,
push you between them,
get on top of you,
stretch the latex, and
talk you through it.

I been traveling to you for four years
from a desperate place
of grimy concrete and oxidized bronze.
I'm tired of assumptions.
Can't you just enter, kneel,
and make me first?
That's why I picked you.

Hard

Dykes are hard
to date.
A dyke wants commitment,
romance without abatement,
and unrelenting virtue—
all before the first show of flesh.
While you, a dyke too (and also hard
to date),
may only want to fuck her,
tell her she's got a nice
back, touch her pussy, talk dirty a little,
she's got another whole agenda.

Dykes should break loose and put off
monogamy, pregnancy, permanency.
Pack your rubber, latex, and leather,
and go on the make.
I know we'll hook up somewhere.

Living as a Lesbian at Forty-Five

Oh, it's a frequent dream:

He (*He?*) comes home hot and
wanting.
You're in your room and wanting too
but wanting to control and orchestrate
so you can get it without really
acknowledging it will have a past
this
one way or another
in concert or in solitude
late
your juices built up from the day
odors sanguine
in the mood to take yourself
you set out your works and toys
and him
even though he knows you're a lesbian
there are those times
he still loses his crotch
in the part of your ass through your dress.

And that's how it happens
and it doesn't happen just once
and you may have work like poetry
to do like now and it starts
making you
pay it
some attention
and you run
and get your accoutrements
in excessive solitude
and space ephemeral with wetness

Najeeb

(1974–1989)

The last Sunday I saw you,
you were so brilliant with light
I could not see your face.
You'd grown taller than me
and were clumsy in your new height
choosing to wear your denim jacket indoors.
Loving your new adolescence, excited by the prospect
of years of growth ahead:
Would you care for me in my old age?
Did I have a right to expect that,
being only an aunt?

Instead I should have held you until you broke away
and even as you broke away.
As it is I cannot remember if I
even touched you as you left
that last Sunday.
You were so brilliant with light
I could not see your face.

Veronica Ashley Wood, My Niece

Welcome, Veronica Ashley Wood.
Vision of god.
Truth.
Your beautiful ten-day-old lips.
What dreams after pain of birth?
We watch you. Feed you.
Pass you among us.
Cry and laugh at your frailty
and the character of your hands.

Hanging Tough in the Persian Gulf

Pvt. Adrienne L. Mitchell, a twenty-three-year-old black woman with a dream, paid a heavy debt for wanting a college degree. Pvt. Mitchell had a goal: a career in law enforcement. She signed up in the army and deferred her duty until she finished her degree. The Gulf War cancelled that deferment, and Pvt. Mitchell found herself in a makeshift barracks in Dahrain, Saudi Arabia, unprized and unknown.

What do mainframe imperialism and a degree in law enforcement have in common? The uniform? In a place nobody knows your name or only knows you as enemy, though history and dark skin make you kin? Pvt. Adrienne L. Mitchell, of Moreno Valley, California, didn't your father tell you he'd lend you the money as he cursed the ball-less wonders on the Hill?

But wasn't Dad a thirty-year veteran and never had a scratch? (And then there was Colin Powell.) That was good enough for you, Adrienne L. Mitchell. You didn't bank on a sho nuff war, in a makeshift barracks, fodder for that Scud the Storm Troopers couldn't cancel. After all you were the daughter of a thirty-year veteran, just trying to pay for a college degree, how could this be?

Elegy

for Donald Woods, 1958–1992

I loved your brown grace and mauve words
from the first night I heard you through
the mist in a Manhattan auditorium.
So like the young redwood, growth inevitable,
its passionate powers,
a poet whose comeliness
I will no longer be able to wrap my arms around.
I fall to pieces and still want your promise
and the sound of your slant voice.
I am not resigned.
You were too quiet.
You sang too low.
How prized if not known?
What would I have done had I known?

an old woman muses from her basement

for Edna Payne Clarke, 1916–2003

there's absolutely no reason (in the world)
nor no need
to go outside again.

i've kinda hoped for this
leveling
to nobody and nothing.
it seems the only honesty possible
without heroes.
rather shabby.
tacky.

no reason (on earth) to go out
unless any of them that's left
outside
comes in here.
ain't likely.
but lord knows i got enough down here
to stock a hotel for a month.
but i'll miss the little runs
to the safeway
papa took me on in the sedan deville

least i'm beginning to pick up static
on the tv.

and papa just went the first thing.
i sewed his easy body in the sheet,
dragged it out to what was his garden.
i look out on him
the sheet more shrunken each day.

me—divorced, two children, the depression,
roosevelt's death.
mccarthy.
the death of billie holiday.
no electricity to no electricity.
i always knew it was all a bum steer.

down here
and old bicycles squealing.
the sudden death of a child
is an awful fact.
good thing i did my big shopping early.
my timing was always perfect.

A Poet's Death

A poet's death and sex thoughts rode me
through the flashing December hurricane.
My day was spent traveling in circles
to get somewhere above ground.
I had a straight-ahead goal when I woke up.
The floods altered it quite a bit.
I didn't get there.
Only got as far as the corner.
The winds and no available cabs
made me turn back.
And I was unfulfilled in the afternoon that followed.

All day long your words fought against my forgetfulness.
They became beasts with sharp bites.
In the distance cars on the FDR were sucked into the East River.
Cum residues sucked me back into thoughts of you.
And you, floating somewhere over the Guinea Coast
or some other blood-anointed place.
And you stuck in Brooklyn,
trains out.

The trains were running by the time I needed to ride
them, and, oh, what a Dutchman's ride they were
with absolutely no service to Far Rockaway.
I did not have to get out of Brooklyn either
and patiently passed the crisis underground.
My addictions tickling me through several stations.
I remembered a poem by Whitman to get my mind
off sugar.

Audre, my good neighbor,
I miss your elegy,
your so-long song,
your striking metonyms,
your hermetic lineation.
Raw and grand images breaking splendidly
and turning to new space.
And spare.
My loveliest, my darkest, my most voice.
I miss my voice, my tongue, my most voluptuous lips.
Totally oblivious of the fact
that a thirty-eight-year-old woman
was killed in Jersey City
struck by a gutter propelled by the winds.
You thought it might have been me.
It might've.

A poet's death and cunt smell
rode me like the angels of hell
on the underground
today
traveling in circles
looking for
vague space somewhere
just ahead or just behind.

Humid Pitch

(1989)

Bulletin

Disguising her vigilance with passive stance, she reads the bulletin stealthily, with some difficulty and great understanding.

> *The General will esteem it as a singular favor if you can apprehend a mulatto girl, servant and slave of Mrs. Washington, who eloped from this place yesterday. She may intend to the enemy. Her name is Charlotte but in all probability will change it. She is light-complected, about thirteen years of age, pert, and dressed in brown cloth westcoat and petticoat. Your falling upon some method of recovering her will accommodate Mrs. Washington and lay her under great obligation to you. A gentle reward will be given to any soldier or other who shall take her up.*

A spray of brown fluid splashes upon the publishing. She tears it down from its post and boot-grinds it into the dirt.

'I bootblacked my face and hands
and any other parts that shows.
Ain't answerin to Charlotte, nigger,
nor no other name they give me.
I'm wearing a westcoat and pants,
left the petticoat in a cornfield.
I'm sixteen. Thirteen was a lie the owner told
the auctioneer.
I'm evil, mean, and will use my knife.
I dips snuff, chews tobacco, smokes a pipe.
Ain't no son of satan gon fall on me lessn
he want his tail curled.
Won't be intendin tward no white folk
—all of ems enemies.
I'm headed west.
I'll swim any river—maybe the Ohio—
follow any star.
And whoever try to take me up
may be ketchin his guts as he run.'

Sisters Part

The men's clothing was a becoming fit
and Justina gave Gatsie the blue stone,
the dark of its matrix
would be diamond by now
in that far place they were forbidden to say.
Forbidden and nearly forgot
on the eve of Gatsie's getting-out time.
The rain would be an awesome shield.
Justina was stern and sharp-eyed.

> 'No time for that lost look.
> Git out now.
> Now while ole woman sick
> and ole man 'fraid to leave her side.
> Don't . . . he'll have his way with you
> You think what he already done bad.
> Wait 'til he git a freer hand.
> Don't think bout nuthin but leavin.'

The stone was the blue of an autumn noon
and the dark of its matrix would be
diamond by now.
Justina was hard and unchangeable.

> 'Come famine, fire, flood, war,
> not goin nowhere.
> Ain't leavin my ghosts.
> You, ya ain't got that kind of company yet.
> You still sleep.
> Day ain't long enough for me . . .
> Go. Leave here.'

Justina smiled.

'Don't come back for me.
Neither send nobody.
Only promise I want
is you leavin.
If ya caught,
swallow what I give ya.'

Gatsie pulled on the hat
and gripped the stone.

party pants

'Ain't nuthin but a house full of mamas and papas, gal.
Tonight I'm a papa.
Sh-sh, don't ya tell nary soul.
Go to my closet.
Gimme them pants I caught you trying on
th'other day.
Yeah.
They fit you right good.
But, no, you ain't wearin em.
Not tonight.
I wears the pants when pants
gots to be worn.
Gimme them suspenders . . .
Honey, now that red shirt
and that pretty black bow tie.
Oh, baby, now my velvet jacket.'

A miracle stood before Star.
Hadn't seen the change herself she
wouldna believed it was Candy but some
exquisite form of man.
But didn't Jesus change water to wine?
Multiply the loaves and fishes?
Raise Laz'rus from the dead?
Raise hisself?
Oh, Mary, don't ya weep
and Martha don't ya moan.

'Get yo hat—the one with the ostrich-tail feather—
smooth yo dress and fasten yo coat.
I like that tight waist.
Take my arm, gal.
Tonight I wanna show you
what I stole you out that field for.'

Frances Michael

Sister Frances Michael was a black nun,
a black nun in a white order.
Not a missionary order or a cloistered
order but a teaching order.
When she wasn't teaching science
she coached basketball.
(Easier since shedding the habit.
Never regained her peripheral vision,
though. But compensation is a nun's way.)

When she wasn't in the gym
or wasn't in the lab,
Frances Michael roamed the halls
with a wide-legged gait and a chip
on her shoulder.
Only Sister Alphonsus, the choir
'directress,' was bold enough to counsel
Frances Michael to tread more straightly
and lightly, to act less arrogantly.
Mother Superior kept to her office
whenever she heard Frances Michael's
brown laughter.

Brainy, brawny, brash Sister Frances Michael.
The white flight girls with their makeup
and hair spray called her the 'Ace of Spades.'
The model black girls who integrated the school
proffered the affectionate ridicule of 'Mike.'
The rowdy, truant girls—a mixed, rag-tag crew,
whose cigarettes and adult books she always took—
called Frances Michael 'Dyke.'

Erol

Erol's van was part art gallery,
juke joint, and mobile home.
The neighbor men bragged about Erol's
serious partyin' in it.

Seventh power of a seventh power,
dazzling the gray-pink dusk.
Saturn of Saturn.

Erol entered a gathering,
everyone—old, blind, or in love—
at once made him welcome, fed him,
held him to her breast,
made him stand back,
admired his heroic looks.

I was an out-of-town neighbor relation
and Erol treated me sweetly because of this
and chivalrously
and did not scorn me like he did
the neighbor men who sought his company.
He showed me the coastline,
the egret, the ibis,
the nesting osprey,
the porpoises at a distance in the grave Atlantic.

'I ain't about gals, baby.'

Did the young men love him
and vie so for his smile and horseplay
because they knew the men he measured them by?
Did the women,
who honored his mother's memory,
who claimed nightly visitations from her,
bring Erol voluptuous fruits,
tender greens from their willing gardens
because they knew his longing?
Did the elder men, who all called him 'Son,'
linger so freely
in the arbor of his awesome hospitality,
his Africanness because they knew?

Didn't we all sit with Erol,
sing with him,
spontaneously touch him,
and copy the way
he twirled a toothpick with his tongue?

Ilona of Hickory

She dreamed of life beyond its crumbling perimeters
     and memorized the rarefied space between the lines of poetry.
Moby-Dick and the Bible whispered their passages to her
     as she rode the train downtown squeezed between philistines.
Ilona of Hickory is a solitary dolphin.

She migrated before the neighborhood changed, before the
     drugs went bad,
          when old women protected the street.
She drank Zinfandel from a jelly jar.

She bid low for the kitty and bid hard
     and laughed when her trump was cut.
Ilona's skill was reading between the leaves.
     Wound like a spiral, Ilona of Hickory,
a goat kicking the mountain she knows loves her,
     a mountain, too, being kicked.

She lived outside, close to the fault.
     Ilona is wisdom in the street
a rose in the woods.

She kisses her enemy's neck
     licks the foamy sea licking her gracious breasts
rescues the child from the hawk.

     Ilona is conscious as a rock.

No Place

This ain't no place to love a woman.
Not a mother.
Surely not a daughter.
Not even some stray mule of a girl-child
whose mama died cursing her pale sire.

The men sang softly and clapped
as we danced.
I withdrew from the circle of women
to also marvel at her supple movement
her wide feet marking rhythm.
I fancied:

She dances for me
and she will lay with me
in this place.

The men clapped for me to dance again.
The women called me back to the circle.

Living as a Lesbian

(1986)

14th Street

was gutted in 1968.
Fire was started on one side of the street.
Flames licked a trail of gasoline to the other side.
For several blocks a gauntlet of flames.
For several days debris smoldered with the stench
of buildings we had known all our lives. Had known
all our lives. I recalled the death of Otis Redding.
My sense of place was cauterized.
Since that time the city has become a buffalo,
nearly a dinosaur, and,
as with everything else white men have wanted
for themselves,
endangered
or extinct.

wearing my cap backwards

poets are among the first witches
so suffer none to live
or suffer none to be heard
and watch them burn before your eyes
'less they recant and speak their verse
in latin.

i'm a poet.
i speaks in pig latin.
i eats pigs feet—a sho nuff sign
of satan
to those whose ears are trained to
dactyls and iambs
who resolve all conflicts in couplets.

i run from mice.
mistake dead, brown leaves
scurried by sharp quick breezes
for rats
and write at stoplights
listening to duke ellington
at the cotton club.

an atavistic witch am i.
wearing beads of tarot
searching for wiccas
burning old drafts
chasing dreaded women
covering their locks
'til sheba's return.

living as a lesbian on the make

Straight bars ain't so bad
though filled with men
cigarette smoke
and juke noises.
A martini straight up and jazz
can take me beyond their static.
Alone she came in denim and a
magenta tee
hair cut to a duck tail
ordered Miller's and smoked two
kinds of cigarettes
sat at a table close but distant
was pretty and I was lonely
and knew she was looking for a woman.
All through the set I looked at her
until she split in the middle of it.
I almost followed her out but was too
horny to leave the easy man talking
loud shit to me for a seduction
I'd have to work at.
The music sounding tasty
saxophone flugelhorn bass and drums
hitting familiar riffs
the names escaping me.

The woman who raised me

asks me
'Where is the hope here, where is the hope?
The fruit here is rotten.
All the roots are excavated.
The sidewalks are cracked and in pieces
and rain forms stagnant pools.
Children walk the night through the streets here
and men make every urge so public.
And who will hear me cry for help?
Will they want to climb all these flights
up here to save me? And what will you do
when you wake up
and find your good woman
gone?'

journal entry: sisters

The two of them are obviously close and not often together.
They give the impression of stolen moments, hidden lives.
The low tones. The tentative eyes.
There is a story to this rendezvous.

The seductive friendliness of the younger-looking one—dyed
dark, too dark, cascading curls, pretty face—offering to light
the cigarette of a stranger at a nearby table.

The quick peripheral glances of the plain, prematurely white-
haired one—younger, tomboyish, near sixty.

They talk very little.
It's their way, to be with one another in whatever way they
can be. And all that's good to be is not necessarily good to
say.

The plain one looks at her neatly clipped nails. The pretty one
surveys surroundings and says: 'I have my grandchildren this
weekend.' The plain one nods and looks downward, over her
shoulder, out the window. 'There's your sister. Better go now,'
says the pretty one making herself small in the booth, offering
the book of matches to the stranger, as her friend slides
past her out of the booth, hurries slump-shouldered to meet
a yet older, more white-haired woman, beckoning for her arm.

for my mother, 1979

My mother lost her right breast and best friend
in two months of one another this winter.
She prepares to lose the first, to sacrifice
the part for the whole.
The second is not even foreshadowed but in
the symbol of the forgone fall.
Severances. Flash floods. Earthquakes.
Lightning rends a tree of its branches.
Unceremoniously abrupt.
To wake on an afternoon to an anesthetized cavity.
Two months later at dawn to news of flames tagging a robe.
The pain of the latter not so splendidly dulled.
And summer is lonely with prosthesis
and surrogate intimacy.

palm leaf of Mary Magdalene

Mary Magdalene's palm leaf to you, dearest whore.
Flash it cross your sex back and forth like a
shoeshine rag more gently with as much dedication
while the one you sleep with tonight instead
of me watches and waits for the miracle.
Tongue of the Holy Ghost
palm leaf of Mary Magdalene.

i come to the city

for protection
and to witness the thick transactions
of women
and women
and dance with my head.
Turns are calculated
to the end on the right foot
to subdue the hip movements.
The city fumes with expectations
and the smells of women
wanting women.
Been in love
six times in the last six months
and ain't done tryin yet.

freedom flesh

for Assata

had you not chosen the dangerous business of
freedom you could be walking barefoot in the
red hills of North Carolina hand in hand with
Kakuya instead of assuming disguises and aliases
traveling through subway stations camping in
sacred aboriginal territory.
you could have been a school marm
community organizer
graduate student
instead of an underground railroad
conductor
picture seen in post offices
or on hastily drafted posters advertising
liberation.

you could have continued giving yourself
guitar lessons
writing political poems
or become a public speaker
instead of ex-political prisoner
paradox   irony   phenomenon
flesh of freedom.

Indira

(1917–1984)

Posed on the bed of an aging, antlike
Gandhi, a Hindu not a Brahmin,
not father nor namesake.
A name you chose, neither Brahmin
nor Hindu.
An aura that confused who you were.
You could have been my own mother
trapped in the violence of some man
she sees every day.
Hostess and harridan.

By sheer dint of rhetoric
saved a Muslim from a lynch mob
in '47, the year I was born.
All noblesse oblige with peasants
pleading their misery to you
in your courtyard daily.
Bright silks drawn tight for protocol.
Princess and dynast.

A rock out of a mob in Orissa!
Nose broken, lip gashed.
Draw your veil over the mess of
blood and pulp.
Refuse to leave the podium.
Victory in Delhi!
A garland of marigolds placed
round your neck by an enemy.
Sit smiling despite your allergy.
Populist and aristocrat.

Two hundred prison letters from
Jawaharlal the Jewel, the democrat,
the atheist you defied in death
with a Hindu funeral
and banned his writings during the
'Emergency.'
Your mother warned you about men,
and you were much in their company.
It's cruel you had only sons, loved
the ruthless one, didn't trust the
other. Who else besides your Sikh
bodyguard knew you wouldn't wear your
vest under orange sari blood-soaked?
Autocrat and pragmatist.

Surrounded by men all your life and
parliaments and cabinets and sycophants.
Nurtured, counseled, schooled, scolded,
ridiculed, and jailed by men, and praying
for the blessings men in power pray for:
    multinationals
    wars
    nukes
    spaceships
    immortality.
Still you could have been a woman in
my own family caught in the violence
of some man in her neighborhood.
Autocrat and despot.

Funeral bier a flotation tank of marigolds.
You in purple sari gold-embellished.
The press could've asked me instead
of Margaret Thatcher how I felt about
your murder—brutal, grisly, male.
After all I've known you all my life.
Black eyes studding the front pages
since before I cared a dark woman
could come to power.

Intimacy no luxury

here.
Telephones cannot be left off the hook
or lines too long engaged
or conversations censored any longer. No
time to stare at our hands
afraid to extend them or once
held
afraid to let go. We are
here.

After years of separation women take
their time
dispose of old animosities.

Ancient panacea, tribadism, cost efficient—
ancient panacea
       cost efficient.

fall journal entry: 1983

Sharon twenty-five
white
wearing pastel bathrobe
pastel nighties
matching terry slippers
from her Riverside window
left thigh
                                        falling

on recently pruned thicket stump
impaled.

No blood from head or mouth
or certain hole.

Rescuers plentiful
and sincere
in earnest
running to each other
with news
and speculation
of ambulances,
an open fourth floor window,
the thing through her thigh.

A woman stroking Sharon
talking soft to her
telling Sharon her name
the names of her children
where she lives
and 'yes, it's gotten chilly . . .'

the doorman old and afraid
bringing blankets.

Sirens all the way
to the river

                            down

fierce and angry
police burning rubber:
         'Who saw what happened here?
                 'Who saw what happened

here?!'
                       'Who saw what happened

here, people?   How can anybody
                     fall

out
of

a
window?'

Blood droplets stain the stump
where medics cut it clean
removing Sharon
gauze wrappings
littering the place where she was.

Who loved Sharon that morning?
Was angry at her?
Hadn't seen her in a long time?
Owed her money?
Who'd she owe money?
Who was she about to make friends with?
Who was on her way over to spend the night?
Was somebody in the room when she
                     fell

jumped
               or was pushed

from her fourth floor
or sixth floor window?
impaled

burst inside
died
holding it all together
on the outside.

sexual preference

I'm a queer lesbian.
Please don't go down on me yet.
I do not prefer cunnilingus.
(There's room for me in the movement.)

Your tongue does not have to prove its prowess
there
to me now
or even on the first night.

Your mouth all over my body
then there.

Miami 1980

Andy Young and Jesse Jackson are summoned to be firemen. In an election year Carter sends his attorney general. The Florida governor pleads only for a night of brotherhood and sends in three thousand five hundred National Guards.

In Vancouver, Washington, not even a forest ranger can be found.

(And what to make of Vernon Jordan shot in Fort Wayne, Indiana, and a mysterious blond who cannot be teased out of seclusion.)

Since Menendez tricked African artisans and agriculturists to settle St. Augustine in 1565, later to be counted among Florida's forty thousand odd slaves—where Maroons and Seminoles protected their vengeance in swamps, where a displaced bourgeoisie can find asylum one hundred years later, a freak place where a ship can destroy a bridge toppling a busload of people to death by water, where an abomination like Anita Bryant can fester and become a Disney World hero—Florida has been a real fantasia.

Jacksonville is the scene of a memorably ruthless episode over lunch counters in 1960 and '64.

Daytona Beach 1926: blacks are made to carry passes after dark.

(However in that same year a hurricane strikes Miami and blacks are forced by armed Marines into the work of reclamation. A black woman is shot by one of them for protesting.)

Miami 1939: men in ritual costume burn twenty-five crosses and parade through the black section carrying effigies and signs spewing: 'the klan will ride again in Florida if niggers try to vote.'

In Tampa 1980 an all-white jury acquits four Miami pigs for beating Arthur MacDuffie to death for forgetting that niggers have no rights white men are bound to respect.

Today sixteen are dead in Miami
and skies are not yet darkened by Mount St. Helens
ending one hundred years of silence with molten rock
burning to ash over western skies
balancing the account.

Miami will stink with unfound corpses
and so will Vancouver, Washington,
so totally surprised a volcano
can find her voice in the fabled new world.

White sidewalks and buildings sprayed with blood
white people claiming innocence of their fathers' transgressions
white women in pin curlers bearing babies and rifles on their
        backs
Arthur MacDuffie's mother begging Liberty City blacks to be
        more long-suffering:
                'Turn to God. Turn to God.'

Liberty City.
Liberty City?

News reports label Miami's violence 'grisly.'
But vengeance is grisly.
The US will die by fire yet.

Living as a Lesbian Underground

In basements attics
alleyways and tents
fugitive slaves poets
and griots discarded
fetuses
Seminoles from Songhay vodun
queens—
all in drag, hitching
dodging state troopers behind shades searching for
safe houses
uptight but cool:
the tam
the aviator frame
the propped cigarette and
singing:
'I was born in Georgia.
My ways are underground. If you
mistreat me,
I'll hunt you like a hound.'

Lack of money produces atavism.

But don't be taken in your sleep now.
Call your assassin's name now.
Leave signs of struggle. Leave
signs of triumph.
And run
cept don't stop in Chicago
to give yourself up to a pimp. Leave
signs.

And don't be taken on the nod now.
Arabs are only a temporary phobia. It's a short
trip from Nyack to the shores of Tripoli and
back. Thewitchhuntisbuildinghere.
Where you gon be when it come?
Leave signs.

And don't get caught sleeping with your
shoes off
while women are forced back to the shelter of
homicidal husbands
rapists are forced to pay child support children of
lesbians orphaned
and blacks, browns, and tans herded into
wire fences somewhere 'round Tucson.
Listen for footsteps.

Leave signs.

Travel light
and don't wait 'til morning.

The terror is here somewhere in
Detroit.

And don't sleep before midnight.
And don't fret over the Poles.
We in the same fix
with the Pope's position on lust and
family protection
a storefront on every corner in
Manhattan.

Don't be a fool, now, cool. Imperialism
by any other name is imperialism.
Even Vietnam was finally over.
It's all the same—

a-rabs, gooks, wogs, queers— a
nigger by any other name . . .
Johannesburg is Jamesburg, New Jersey.
Apartheid is the board of education in
Canarsie.

So, don't be taken in your sleep now.
Call your assailant's name now.
Leave the building empty the
doors unlocked
and raise the windows high when
they pass by.
Leave signs of struggle.

Leave signs of triumph.

Leave signs.

An exile I have loved

tells me
she's going home.
Smug I say:
        'Back to the city?'
        'No. First to Zambia. Then Zimbabwe.
        Finally Transvaal. Home,' she answers, sad.
We sleep and wake to voices of men in the hallway
asking through doors of faces that are changed
and names that have not been spoken since.
I hold her to me
ask for a way to stay in touch with her
tell her she's got a home long as I got mine.
Hold her to me until she must push away

slip

from the room.

sister of famous artist brother

a bizarre poetry—tabloids
cash register receipts
but less honest
never the sum
always the part.
hadn't been for 'famous artist brother's'
name dominating the coverage
might not have known you were
stabbed to death in 'posh pad.'
and whose business was it anyway
how you got to live in manhattan plaza?
KIMAKO BARAKA   SONDRA ELAINE   JONES

reached back twenty years in famous
artist brother's life. only the last
twenty minutes of yours titillated
their imaginations.
he won an obie.
you sold amway.
they sell pulp.
and can't even say your name
'cept to say his first.
SONDRA ELAINE   KIMAKO BARAKA   JONES

i start at noises i hear every night
and don't want to be sleeping by myself
and call other women i know who live alone.

a day later:
twenty-nine-year-old klansman sentenced to death
for beating   strangling   hanging
nineteen-year-old black man two years before
'to show klan strength in alabama.'

not quite so amazing
as the twenty-one-year-old sadistic waif
you befriended
tried to save
two weeks before he grabbed you
round the neck by your shirt
drove a household knife
in your chest
deep in your head
and how'd you get to live in a
'luxury high-rise' anyway?
KIMAKO   SONDRA ELAINE   BARAKA   JONES

grimly famous artist brother, roi, asks:
'is this the way it happened?'
remembering perhaps mocking you in
Home.
you danced acted wrote directed
dreamed right on

proselytizer
entrepreneur
cultural worker
fighter—
put up a 'ferocious struggle'
leaving 'swank manhattan pad
a shambles.'
and how'd you get to live there anyway
being only 'strayed,' 'little' sister
of famous artist brother
only SONDRA ELAINE JONES
only a black woman
KIMAKO?

Kittatinny

I wanna love and treat, love and treat you right.

—BOB MARLEY, "IS THIS LOVE?"

Kittatinny Tunnel in that holy place you let me hit
I push on toward your darker part.
I'll take you there and mean it.

In my car, by the road, in a tent, in a pit
stop, and practice a funkier art,
Kittatinny Tunnel of that holy place you let me hit.

Shout, cry, promise, beg, cajole, go limp, or spit
on me with dirty words to test my heart.
I'll take you there and mean it.

Crawl from me, pitch a fit,
stand, hug the wall, bend, and direct me part
and penetrate Kittatinny, that holy place you let me hit.

And take it, take it, take it.
Call it bitch, whore, slave, tart.
I'll take you there and mean it.

Tribad, dildo, lick your clit-
oris. Come, pee, shit, or fart,
I'll take you there and mean it,
Kittatinny Tunnel of that holy place you let me hit.

living as a lesbian at thirty-five

in my car I am fishing in my pocketbook
eyes on the road
for my wallet.
in my mind I am fishing in your drawers
eyes on the road
for your pussy.
high speeds evoke fucking.
depending on your mood you come.
it goes on:
I do too from you
over the wheel
hand between my thighs
eyes on the road
and the end of all

my mind:
a favored child has more freedom from her parents
a hippocampus more freedom from the horse and dolphin
a hippopotamus more freedom from her short legs
and muzzle
than my hypothalmus from lusting
and the end of all.

my age?
the years I missed?
the women I had no opportunity with?
an old lover is sweet and good.
an old friend surprising and familiar.
all bodies possibilities.
any bodies.
lust, the cause of every tribute and transaction
for the end of all.

to work to the end of day
to talk to the end of talk
to run to the end of dark
to have at the end of it all.

the wish for forever
for more often
for more.
promises
absurdity
histrionics
loss of pride
bargaining
sadness after.

in wakefulness wanting
in wakefulness waiting.

Narratives: poems in the
tradition of black women

(1982)

Of Althea and Flaxie

In 1943 Althea was a welder
very dark
very butch
and very proud
loved to cook, sew, and drive a car
and did not care who knew she kept company with a woman
who met her every day after work
in a tight dress and high heels
light-skinned and high-cheekboned
who loved to shoot, fish, play poker
and did not give a damn who knew her 'man' was a woman.

Althea was gay and strong in 1945
and could sing a good song
from underneath her welder's mask
and did not care who heard her sing her song to a woman.

Flaxie was careful and faithful
mindful of her Southern upbringing
watchful of her tutored grace
long as they treated her like a lady
she did not give a damn who called her 'bulldagger.'

In 1950 Althea wore suits and ties.
Flaxie's favorite colors were pink and blue.
People openly challenged their flamboyance
but neither cared a fig who thought them 'queer' or 'funny.'

When the girls bragged over break of their sundry loves,
Flaxie blithely told them her old lady Althea took her dancing
every weekend and did not give a damn
who knew she clung to a woman.

When the boys on her shift complained of their wives,
Althea boasted of how smart her 'stuff' Flaxie was
and did not care who knew she loved the mind of a woman.

In 1955 when Flaxie got pregnant
and Althea lost her job
Flaxie got herself on relief
and did not care how many caseworkers
threatened midnight raids.

Althea was set up and went to jail
for writing numbers in 1958.
Flaxie visited her every week with gifts
and hungered openly for her through the bars
and did not give a damn who knew she waited for a woman.

When her mother died in 1965 in New Orleans
Flaxie demanded that Althea walk beside her in the funeral procession
and did not care how many aunts and uncles knew she slept with a woman.

When she died in 1970
Flaxie fought Althea's proper family not to have her laid out in lace
and dressed the body herself
and did not care who knew she made her way with a woman.

Mavis writes in her journal

. . . I know Geneva loves me
more than the man she sleeps with every night
and still our conversation is reduced
from talk of world events to
news of the latest white sale
whenever he blunders into the kitchen
for a toothpick.

. . . Geneva can't tell him the same secrets she tells me.

He draws the blood. I know the scars. I acknowledge her mind.
He ignores her body and makes her sense a dartboard.

. . . Why is it we never act on our own hunger?

Yesterday we were listening to Billie Holiday sing
'Practice Makes Perfect' when Geneva lost track of time, rushed home to cook
his dinner . . . Men learn to be chefs and short order cooks
but never learn to feed themselves.

. . . I am patient and relentless.

Today I kissed Geneva full on the lips and today for the first time
she asked me to leave when he came home from work and went straight
to the icebox for a beer, grunting at us as he popped the cap, exploding
the contents all over Geneva's highly polished linoleum.

. . . Our touches were tentative at first, then there was confidence,
and passion, and wonder . . . then fear.

. . . He's too sure of his cock ever to suspect it will be supplanted.
Tonight Geneva keeps him company.
Tonight I write another brazen love poem in secret, alone, patient,
and relentless.

The Older American

Lettie Walker was seventy-one
when she was struck unconscious in the street
by a hit-and-run driver
who seemed not to have obeyed the stop sign
or perhaps became impatient with her halt gait.

Mrs. Walker,
a widow
long past the empty-nest syndrome
living alone
prone to speak symbolically
metaphorically
biblically
content in having only to do for self,
did not die.
She lay at the curb unbloody for nearly an hour
before anyone noticed her body.

At the hospital she regained her sense of things.
A youngish, white-coated white man
asked Mrs. Walker how she felt.
Laughing, Mrs. Walker said: 'Like a leaf.'

'What happened?' the man continued, chagrined.

'They crucified Jesus. They only hit me with a car.'

Considering her color, her age, her seeming disorientation,
and that no pocketbook had been recovered,
the man presumed Mrs. Walker to be a cast-off thing
and probably a little demented.

After applying several pokes and squeezes to her rather vulnerable body
the man ordered x-rays
and the next thing she knew
Mrs. Walker was going under in the o.r. for something called 'exploratory.'

Since that time
Lettie Walker has been depressed
agoraphobic
nearly anorexic
taken to walking with a cane
given up her home in the South
to stay with her daughter in the North
and ambivalent about wanting to live.

Fathers

My father, a child himself,
once defied the law
and asked me what I told the priest.

I snap coyly that he is not the *father*
I am sworn to tell my sins to.

He is relentlessly sweet as a pedophile.

I succumb
give him details of my most recent confession
juicy with childish improprieties.

The seal of secrecy is broken.
But I preferred guilt to grace anyhow.

Grace is amazing
She is lean and tight in her flesh.
A gymnast and a dancer.
She is my sister.
Her father, not the sweet child mine is,
never lives with us.
I see him pass our street in his green Buick convertible
looking askance
for a glance
of my mother or Grace.

But Grace . . .
amazing is the only word for her.

My mother loved Grace
and required nothing of her.
And berated me,

dark, short-haired, big for my age.
But Grace . . . amazing
she never required anything of her.
Only monotonously brushed and braided
her long, thick brown hair,
while assaulting me with straightening irons.

Grace was never blamed for her diminished likeness to the West Afrikan
the way I was blamed for diminishing my mother's
two generations removed caucaso-indio bloodlines.

Grace was never required to be anything but amazing.

Even after she had my father's baby at fourteen
Grace could still turn cartwheels
do headstands
and dance the stomp 'til dawn
smiling furtively at me
holding my nephew
my brother
holding the secret of the union
that bore him
and binds us.

The Moon in Cancer

The moon is orange tonight and sandwiched between charcoal clouds.
Rachel is Cancer
tropical and lovable
fluid and mean.
Unlike me
earthbound and melancholy
indulging and always freely singing
some woman-sung
old didactic doo-ah:

> *understanding is something that makes everything just fine.*
> *I'll never be contented 'til you say that you are mine.*

The moon is orange and makes crabs scuttle
scuttle from sand
sometimes to cobblestone.
Rachel is Cancer
charismatic and self-contained
gregarious and predatory.
Not like me
who under the night's reflection in her window
nightly and loudly sang
some old settlin down song:

> *don't drift too far baby, stick around and stay near.*

The street made Rachel's time.
And me trying to mime its joyful and desperate rhyme.
Never once did she celebrate in my ear
the promise of some old unauthored
woman-sung refrain:

> *I'm gonna straighten up and fly right and*
> *and quit my raising sand.*

And me loudly singing to the crescent moon
of her hidden circumference,
and boldly changing nouns and pronouns
for her so she could hear the wisdom
of some old woman-sung advice:

> *girls, if you got a good woman*
> *better keep her by your side.*
> *cause if she flag my train,*
> *I'ma sure let her ride.*

But Rachel is Cancer
tropical, lovable,
fluid,
charismatic, self-contained,
gregarious, predatory
and mean.
Unlike me
who only ever wanted
Rachel between me
like the moon
orange and sandwiched between
charcoal clouds.

Gail

Gail, Gail.
Chicago nightingale
bred on blues and Bigger Thomas
and extreme weather.
Lover of cocaine and marijuana
on tropical and early mornings in summer
and *One Hundred Years of Solitude* in winter.

Gail
toucan and nightingale.
Sitting reading Jung in a Newark food stamp office
and speaking in dreams of atavistic masks.

Gail
girl mother.
Brushing, braiding other women's daughters' hair between your thighs
before that marauding time of womb-swelling, scraping, and pillage.

Gail
plumèd amazon.
Tearing up diary pages filed in boxes and drawers crowded with
scents and sachets
singing r&b in Spanish
beating out a latin two-step
with your fist.

Gail, Gail
midwest nightingale in an eastbound flight.

hair: a narrative

it is passing strange to be in the company
of black women
and be the only one who does not worry about
not being with a man
and even more passing strange
is to be among black women
and be the only one wearing her hair natural
or be the only one who has used a straightening iron

An early childhood memory:

me: sitting in the kitchen holding down
onto my chair shoulders hunching
toes curling.

my mother: standing behind me
bracing herself against the stove
greasing the edges of my scalp
and the roots of my hair violently
heating the straightening comb alternately
and asking between jerking and pulling:

    'why couldn't you have *good* hair?'

by the time mother finished pressing my virgin wool
to patent leather,
I was asking why I had to have hair at all.

(the first time I heard a straightening iron crackle through my
greased kitchen, I thought a rattlesnake had got loose.)

so much pain to be black, heterosexual, and female
to be trained for some *Ebony* magazine mail order man
wanting a woman with long hair, big legs, and able
to bear him five sons.
hardly any man came to be worth the risk of nappy edges.

the straightening iron: sado-masochistic artifact salvaged
from some chamber of the Inquisition and given new purpose
in the putative new world.

what was there
about straight hair
that made me want to suffer
the anguishes of hell
to have it?
made me a recluse
on any rainy, snowy, windy, hot, or humid day,
away from any activity that produced the least
moisture to the scalp.
most of all sex.
(keeping the moisture from my scalp
always meant more to me
than fucking some dude.)

there was not
a bergamot
or a plastic cap
that could stop
water
from undoing
in a matter of minutes
what it had taken hours of torture
to almost perfect.
I learned to hate water.

I am Virgo and pragmatic
at fifteen I made up my mind
if I had to sweat my hair back with anyone

it would be my beautician.
she made the pretense bearable.

once a month I would wait several hours
in that realm of intimacy
for my turn in her magical chair
for my four vigorous shampoos
for her nimble fingers to massage
my hair follicles to arousal
for her full bosom to embrace
my willing head
against the war of tangles
against the burning metamorphosis
she touched me naked
taught me art
gave me good advice
gave me language
made me love something about myself.

Willie Mays's wife thought integration
meant she could get a permanent in a
white woman's beauty salon
and my beautician telling me to love myself
applying the chemical
careful of the time
soothing me with endearments
and cool water to stop the burning
then the bristle rollers
to let me dry forever
under stacks of *Jet, Tan,* and *Sepia,*
and then the magnificence of the comb-out.

'au naturel' and the promise of
black revolutionary cock a la fanon
made our relationship suspect.
I asked for tight curls.
my beautician gave me a pick
and told me no cock was worth so drastic a change.

I struggled to be liberated from the supremacy
of straight hair,
stopped hating water
gave up the desire for the convertible sports coup
and applied the lessons of my beautician
who never agreed with my choice
and who nevertheless still gives me language, art,
intimacy, good advice,
and four vigorous shampoos per visit.

ACKNOWLEDGMENTS

Profound and heartfelt thanks are extended to Dr. Julie R. Enszer, editor and publisher of *Sinister Wisdom*, which publishes the work of numerous lesbian feminist writers, including the 2014 reprint of my 1986 book of poetry, *Living as a Lesbian*. Julie has been editing, publishing, and promoting my work for nearly twenty years. Much appreciation is also extended to my old friend, the poet Cheryl Boyce-Taylor, for introducing me to Parneshia Jones at Northwestern University Press, who embraced me and my work from the beginning. To writers Breena Clarke, my sister, and Esther Cohen, my dear comrade, I am grateful for weekly, scintillating conversations about our writing. Happily, I thank the incomparable Barbara Balliet, scholar, bookseller, and life partner, for making my life so beautiful for an extraordinary thirty-two years.

NOTES

New Poems

+ **Jo'burg, 2016**
Nie-Blanke translates from Afrikaans as "non-white." *Blanke* and *Nie-Blanke* ticket holders see different presentations of the same material. This, of course, is a smart attempt to allow patrons to experience briefly the emotional ache of racial separation. What if my friend Zee and I had been given different tickets?!

ANC (African National Congress), founded in 1912, is the revolutionary party that spearheaded the breakdown of Apartheid and has been the ruling party in South Africa since 1994. PAC (the Pan African Congress) was founded in 1959, when it broke away from ANC and advocated a South Africa based on black nationalism. SWAPO (South West Africa People's Organisation) was founded in 1960 in Namibia as the party of liberation (and is still the ruling party there). UDF (United Democratic Front, 1983–1991) was an umbrella group of four hundred public organizations that fought for a "nonracial" South Africa; and MK (uMkhonto we Sizwe) was a paramilitary arm of ANC, established in 1961 after the sixty-nine murders of black South Africans in Sharpeville in 1961.

+ **Sandy Bland**
Sandra Bland was a young black woman stopped by white state trooper Brian Encinia in Prairie View, Texas, in 2015. He began to follow Bland, who moved to the right to let him pass. He stopped her because she did not signal. During the stop, she had the temerity to light a cigarette, which he ordered her to extinguish. The encounter led to Bland's arrest, jailing, and three days later her death, ruled suicide.

Good? Dialogue cited from Malcolm Gladwell's odd book, *Talking to Strangers*.

+ **Missed Love**
Reprinted from *Ten: Hobart Festival of Women Writers, Tenth Anniversary Collection* (Bushel Editions, 2023).

+ Uvalde, Texas, May 24, 2022

"Pretend to sleep, baby" is what a grandmother, Felicia Sanders, one of the three survivors of the Charleston, South Carolina, church massacre on June 17, 2015, said to her five-year-old granddaughter, Polly Sheppard, as they pretended to be dead.

+ Mother Emanuel Nine: their influence was wide

My Jersey City neighbor, Ms. Florence Holmes, is from Charleston, South Carolina, and, as a youngster, knew Ms. Susie Jackson, the oldest person murdered in that massacre. Ms. Holmes exclaimed to me, "We knew that woman, Cheryl. Ms. Susie Jackson. We used to call, 'Miss Susie,' to her every day as we passed by on our way to school." See Jelani Cobb, "Murders in Charleston," *New Yorker*, June 18, 2015. Cobb himself encountered a flight attendant with whom he struck up a conversation on the massacre and who knew personally one of the nine—"their influence was wide."

Selected Poems

Targets

+ Targets

The target-practice story had come to light after National Guard Sgt. Valerie Deant saw bullet-riddled mugshots of black men at a police shooting range. One photo was of Deant's brother. She complained. Outrage followed in North Miami Beach and beyond as critics called for the police chief's resignation. See Elahe Izadi, "Florida Police Used Mugshots of Black Men for Target Practice. Clergy Responded: #UseMeInstead," *Washington Post*, January 25, 2015.

+ Open Heart Surgery

Deep gratitude first of all to Maury Collins, my high school classmate and Chicagoan (via DC), for saving my life by driving me to the ER at the University of Chicago Medical Center. Thanks to Dr. Takeyoshi Ota and the Chicago Med Cardiac Team, who performed the open heart surgery on April 10, 2017. Serious gratitude to my dear brother-in-law, David Balliet, for driving us from Chicago to his and his wife Nancy's house in Chestertown, Maryland, where I began recuperating. Thanks to everyone who supported Barbara and me during my recovery. Eternal love and thanks to

Barbara Balliet, who, from the beginning, got me through recuperation and recovery.

+ **Woman Ends Her Life: Elegy**
The epigraph is from a 1911 obituary in the *Delaware County Times*.

By My Precise Haircut

+ **Mandela: 12-5-2013**
Marc Crawford (1929–1996) was a journalist for *Ebony, Jet*, and *Freedom-ways*, and the first black journalist for *Life* magazine. He was also a teacher, author, and cultural critic. He covered very dangerous civil rights protests and struggles leading to arrests and police brutality. During one arrest, he was kicked in the teeth for his participation and coverage of the struggle. Of course Mandela was in jail for life at the time I knew Marc in the early 1970s as a faculty-person at Livingston College (Rutgers University) in Piscataway, New Jersey. Marc was a really wild brilliant man. I don't know if he made it to Mandela's release in 1990. Keorapetse W. Kgositsile (1938–2018) was a South African poet and political activist and an influential member of the African National Congress (ANC), who was in exile in the United States from 1962 to 1975 and joined the Black Arts Movement. Sometimes called "Willie," he published poetry with Broadside Lotus Press, the major independent press propagating the poetry of the movement. Broadside, founded by Dudley Randall (1914–2000), was located in Detroit. So many men here.

+ **a capital car chase**
The dedication to Miriam Carey refers to the thirty-four-year-old dental hygienist and mother who drove her black Infiniti through the police barricades and onto the grounds of the White House on October 3, 2013. The Secret Service ordered her to stop, but she continued driving at high speeds through downtown DC traffic toward the Capitol grounds, then backing up into another vehicle. She was shot five times in the back. She died. Miraculously, her one-year-old daughter survived. Her family filed a wrongful death suit, after the US Attorney for Washington, DC, found that excessive force was not used. I guess we all remember the man from Texas who in 2014 was able to climb a fence in front of the White House and enter the front door, concealing a knife, who was merely arrested.

- Women of Letters

  Belinda, a slave in the Royall House, wrote a petition to the Common-wealth of Massachusetts in 1783, requesting an income from the estate of her former owner, Isaac Royall. See also Rita Dove's poem, "Belinda's Petition."

  "Letter from a close friend written four days after you die and received three days after your birthday," is in memory of my aunt, Hannah T. Logan (Oct. 23, 1894–April 18, 1967).

The Days of Good Looks: 2000–2005

- james dean longing

  Jerome Johnson (1946–1972) was from New Brunswick, NJ, where and why I first and last met him, because I lived there from 1969 to 1997, and he was related to my close male friend. In Central Park, Johnson was gunned down by bodyguards of Mafioso Joe Columbo after he shot and killed the Don.

Experimental Love

- Greta Garbo

  Thanks to the late and beautiful Mr. Lee Dobson and my dear cousin Ms. Barbara Clarke, New York City actors, for the story behind "Please, do you have men's pajamas?" They were both retailers at high-end clothing stores in Manhattan, who could claim the distinction of having waited on Garbo.

- Movement

  Parts of "Movement" are influenced by Taylor Branch's *Parting the Waters: America in the King Years 1954–63* (New York: Simon and Schuster, 1988); John Blassingame's *Slave Testimony* (Baton Rouge: Louisiana State University Press, 1977); and *The Life of Olaudah Equiano* (1789) in *The Classic Slave Narratives*, edited by Henry Louis Gates Jr. (New York: New American Library, 1987).

- Flowers of Puerto Rico

  Epigraph by Frances E. W. Harper is from "Black Women in the Recon-struction South" in *Black Women in White America: A Documentary History*, edited by Gerda Lerner (New York: Vintage Books, 1973).

  "Reina de las Flores" is influenced by Adrienne Kennedy's *Electra* in *In One Act* (Minneapolis: University of Minnesota Press, 1988).

- Querida

    In *Experimental Love*, this poem appears under the title "Dear One."

- Hard

    In *Experimental Love*, this poem is titled "Dykes Are Hard."

- Hanging Tough in the Persian Gulf

    See "For Some Military Presented a Path to College Degree," *Washington Post*, Sunday, March 10, 1991, p. A22.

Humid Pitch

- Bulletin

    The italicized passage is taken from Frank R. Stockton, "The Slaves of New Jersey," in *Stories of New Jersey* (New Brunswick: Rutgers University Press, 1961). This book was originally published in 1896. The passage was reproduced by Stockton from a letter (c. 1776) written by one of George Washington's aides to a friend in Elizabethtown (Elizabeth, New Jersey) on Washington's behalf when Washington was stationed in nearby Morristown. Charlotte's response is the poet's fiction.

- party pants

    This poem is an excerpt from the much longer poem, "Epic of Song," which is a fictive treatment of the lives of Ma Rainey and her acolyte Bessie Smith.

- Ilona of Hickory

    This poem was drawn from a reading of Jesse Cougar's *A Poet's Tarot* (1986), particularly these cards: XII of Sticks, XIII of Sticks, Eternity, I of Pens, III of Pens, Cataclysm—The Revolutionary, VI of Bowls, and VIII of Knives.

Living as a Lesbian

- i come to the city

    The conclusion of this poem is adapted from blues songs sung by Bessie Smith, 1925–1927. *Bessie Smith: Nobody's Blues But Mine* (Columbia Records; reissued 1972).

- Miami 1980

  "Miami 1980": A reference to the riots in Miami following the acquittal of the four white police officers in the killing of Arthur McDuffie, a black insurance salesman and Marine Corps corporal.

- Living as a Lesbian Underground

  The lines "I was born in Georgia . . . I'll hunt you like a hound" are adapted from "Honey Man Blues" as sung by Bessie Smith.

- An exile I have loved

  The line "got a home as long as I got mine" is adapted from "I Left My Baby" from the album *Jimmy Rushing: Sent for You Yesterday* (Bluesway, reissued 1973).

- sister of famous artist brother

  This poem was first published in 1986. Though Kimako Baraka's given name has been spelled both "Sandra" and "Sondra" and her middle name has been alternately given as "Elaine" and "Lee," I have used "Sondra Elaine Jones" for the past thirty-eight years. See Baraka's 1961 irreverent poem, "Lanie Poo," written for his sister, and his reference to her in his eulogy:

  > my sister was brutally murdered beaten to death stabbed to death by an insane reflection of the real american dream which is a nightmare . . . we will not be intimidated even by the wanton destruction of this life so close to our hearts. We see here the way she looked. *Sandi. Laine. Laney. Lanie Poo. Kimako.* https://unityarchiveproject.org/article/lanie-poo-remember -kimako-baraka/